Stress Management For Life

Manage Your Stress and Social Anxiety, Overcome Your Depression and Addiction for Mental Peace and Improving Relationships, Practicing Minimalism and Meditation

By

Paul Adams

© **Copyright 2018 by Paul Adams**

All rights reserved.

The content contained within this book may not be reproduced, duplicated or transmitted without direct written permission from the author or the publisher.

Under no circumstances will any blame or legal responsibility be held against the publisher, or author, for any damages, reparation, or monetary loss due to the information contained within this book. Either directly or indirectly.

Legal Notice:

This book is copyright protected. This book is only for personal use. You cannot amend, distribute, sell, use, quote or paraphrase any part, or the content within this book, without the consent of the author or publisher.

Disclaimer Notice:

Please note the information contained within this document is for educational and entertainment purposes only. All effort has been executed to present accurate, up to date, and reliable, complete information. No warranties of any kind are declared or implied. Readers acknowledge that the author is not engaging in the rendering of legal, financial, medical or professional advice. The content within this book has been derived from various sources. Please consult a licensed professional before attempting any techniques outlined in this book.

By reading this document, the reader agrees that under no circumstances is the author responsible for any losses, direct or indirect, which are incurred as a result of the use of information contained within this document, including, but not limited to, — errors, omissions, or inaccuracies.

Table of Contents

Introduction 8

    Sources of Stress 11

Chapter 1: The Science of Stress 13

    Types of Stress 14

    Self-Assessment Test 18

Chapter 2: Power of Perception 22

    Tips and Strategies 25

Chapter 3: Mindfulness 34

    A Few Noteworthy Things about Mindfulness 36

    Cultivating Mindfulness 38

Chapter 4: Importance of Values 46

    Types of Values 46

    Why Are They Important 48

    Defining Values 52

Chapter 5: Spirituality 57

    Better Decision-Making 58

    Longevity 59

    Forgiveness 59

    Peace 60

Giving Up Control 62

Finding the Lesson 62

Resilience 63

Spirituality and Stress Relief 65

Discovering Spirituality 67

Cultivating Spirituality 68

Chapter 6: Meditation 70

Benefits of Meditation 70

Meditation Prerequisite 72

How to Meditate 75

Guided Meditation 83

Chapter 7: Quick Fix for Stress 85

Try to Engage in Physical Activities 85

Laugh 88

Talk 90

Write it Down 91

Music 92

Pet an Animal 96

Play a Mind Game 100

Hug 100

Acupressure 104

- Cry 106
- Lavender Scent 108

Chapter 8: More Ways to Reduce Stress 110

- Time and Tasks Management 110
- Allocating Some Time for Breaks 112
- Relaxation Techniques 115
- Get Enough Sleep 116
- Avoid Consuming Alcohol, Nicotine, and Caffeine ... 119
- Maintain a Healthy Diet 122
- If All Else Fails, Seek a Specialist 125

Chapter 9: Progressive Muscle Relaxation 127

- PMR: Step by Step 128

Chapter 10: Social Support 131

- Benefits of Social Support 131
- Types of Social Support 132
- Nurturing the Social Network 134

Chapter 11: Common Mistakes During Stress 136

- Making Hasty Decision 136
- Procrastinate 137
- Isolation 139
- Taking No Break 139

Not Accepting Reality 140

Conclusion 141

Introduction

Mankind is the most evolved species, both physically and intelligently, amongst other species on Earth. At the same time, they are also known to be the busiest and brightest species in control of the world. The world as we know it is changing quickly and everyone has started to think more and more, making life slowly but steadily become more complicated. People worry about every little thing and put themselves in difficult situations that hinder their enjoyment in their precious lives. These behaviors are highly detrimental to their mental health.

Nowadays, performance is key in every professional environment. Everyone needs to keep their performance at its peak and keep up with competitors, or otherwise be left in the dust. As the professional environment becomes more and more competitive, work begins taking its toll on everyone's health.

Young people are most influenced by this increase in competition. They strive to be the best just because they want to relax on a Sunday afternoon without having to worry about what to eat tomorrow, or the fact that they still do not have enough money to pay last month's bill. The situation for them is slowly getting worse and worse. They often complain about how they are losing focus on their tasks. The damage to their mental health is often overlooked, and it all starts with stress.

Unlike the old days, when work was often limited to physical labor, modern work involves the use of your intellectual skills and power. This creates the belief that work is health obsolete. Now, society and the workplace everyone works in places an unprecedented amount of pressure on everyone. Stress is so common nowadays that everyone has come to embrace it, as well as the debilitating consequences it brings.

According to an annual survey on stress conducted by the American Psychological Association in 2011, almost 25% of respondents reported their stress at the extreme level. About 40% stated that their stress had gone up in the past year, and up to 45% said that it had increased in the past five years. Plus, there was a consensus that stress, more or less, had negative impacts on the quality of their lives. Unfortunately, many people believe that stress is only psychological, meaning it does not affect your physical wellbeing. However, experts across medical disciplines all believe that this is a misconception (and a very dangerous one).

According to Rick Hanson, Ph.D., a neuropsychologist, modern life exposes everyone to stress, varying from mild to moderate stress, but all are chronic nonetheless. The common sources are multitasking, handling too many things at the same time, moving around too fast, or simply receiving too much stimulation.

Stress is one of the commonly used terms in modern society. There are several definitions of stress, and they vary slightly based on their context. The most popular definition is that stress is a situation in which there is an emotional or mental strain or tension happening in the body as a result of demanding circumstances.

This book is intended to provide insights, not only on how to manage stress, but also how to improve the quality of life by addressing personal problems such as social anxiety, depression, and addiction, not to mention how to improve relationships and achieve mental peace. The goal of this book is to help people who are struggling in their daily life to overcome their problem and achieve more with fewer problems. The main source of all of mankind's problem stems from stress, and it needs to be addressed before one can achieve anything.

Stress is indiscriminate, meaning that it affects everyone regardless of social group or age. Everyone will experience stress at some point during their lives. Some will have it worse than others. So, where does stress come from?

Sources of Stress

Stress is a natural response from our body to daily events. Although there are many sources of stress and equally as many ways to react to it, stress is a human's defense mechanism. In ancient times, stress helped us survive in a wilderness full of predators. Now, the purpose of stress is almost irrelevant. Stress is indeed natural, in a sense that stressful situations are expected to resolve quickly, which is helpful in the wild for both predator and prey. In modern society, the human body does not understand the current situation. When a person feels stressful, their body is led to believe that they are experiencing danger for 8 or even 10 hours a day. It is clearly not designed to handle that level of stress since the natural biological, evolutionary design is to have some periods of recovery after bursts of stress. Therefore, it is advisable for individuals to take control of themselves when stress weighs them down.

Sources of stress can be categorized into various groups such as social, emotional, physical, psychological, etc. Stress can be caused by joyous moments, such as weddings, births, travel, or winning the lottery. On the other hand, events such as getting fired, divorced, dumped, or a loved one's death can also cause stress. Whatever the event may be, the effect can also vary from being minor to very significant, and its effect can be as quick as a few hours, or it can haunt individuals for the rest of their lives, in some cases. So, how does a person's body react to stress?

Chapter 1: The Science of Stress

When you feel stressful, hormones begin to surge through your body. Those hormones are adrenaline and cortisol, and they come from the bottom part of the brain known as the hypothalamus. They aid you in dealing with pressure or threats that you face, commonly known as the "fight or flight" response. Here, the adrenaline increases your heart rate, your blood pressure, and gives the person the extra energy they might need to fight or run away from the threat.

On the other hand, Cortisol, which is commonly known as the stress hormone, increases your energy temporarily by allowing glucose to be released into the bloodstream, which also gives a person the energy to fight or run. While those two hormones work to prepare the body for action, other bodily functions such as digestion are temporarily suppressed because they are not needed. Most of the time, the body always regulates stress on its own. Once the threat is gone, the blood pressure and heart rate will return to normal.

In a way, stress stimulates our body. We all need a healthy dose of stress or pressure to live a healthy life, not to mention that they keep our performance at peak efficiency. After all, stress is what gets many people out of bed every morning and keeps one motivated throughout the day.

Types of Stress

Many people believe that stress is a bad thing. However, given the right circumstances, stress can motivate you to do more and promote self-growth. The key here is to keep the stress at an optimal level. What is the difference between good and bad stress?

Good Stress

As mentioned earlier, stress can come from a happy source. Good stress, or eustress, works by compelling everyone to achieve their goals, resulting in happiness, success, or fulfillment. Eustress normally come in the form of short bursts that gives everyone just the energy they need to finish a job or get over an obstacle. It is something that the person is excited about, and common causes of eustress are a deadline, a test, or a speech. Here, eustress has been shown to enhance learning and brain functions as well. Eustress does not last long enough to cause any damage, and is overall beneficial to everyone as it has been since ancient times.

To illustrate, suppose that a deadline draws near. Eustress comes into play by helping the individual focus on his work and perform well, granting the chance to recover from the stress. Then, it is clear that there is an increase in performance. However, if the person struggles to meet deadline after deadline, regardless of how they try to prepare, then their performance may take a hit. If they have no time to recover, then this eustress or good stress turns into bad stress.

Bad Stress

Bad stress is characterized as chronic or ongoing stress. It can slow an individual down and prevent them from doing things they need or want to do. This negative stress is detrimental because one never has a chance to recover from the fight-or-flight effect. When someone is constantly threatened, their body and performance suffer, and the benefit of stress is lost.

When a person is going through stress, the reproductive, immune, digestive, and excretory systems cannot return to a normal state so long as the "threat" remains. The person will find it hard to focus and becomes irritable, depressed, etc. Stress is also commonly linked to heart disease, weight gain, and more. The longer the stress lasts, the higher the risk. Chronic stresses are linked to some common events, such as relationship troubles, high demand at work, and loss of a loved one.

Here, the type of stress depends on the amount to which a person is exposed. Too little or too much stress is still bad for the body.

The lack of stress means that the body is under-stimulated. On the other hand, prolonged stress that is too intense can be damaging to the body. The latter leads to headaches, stomach problems, or high blood pressure. In some extreme cases, stress can even cause a stroke or heart attack.

Most of the time, psychological problems are caused by stress. Anger, anxiety, fear, or distrust are linked to stress. This can destroy relationships both at home and in the workplace. Moreover, stress can even weaken your immune system, making you prone to some preventable diseases.

While the causes of stress are grasped, and its functions understood, one needs to recognize that stress is there to take action. Here are a few ways to diagnose if stress is present in the body.

Self-Assessment Test

In this test, several observations need to be made from various angles. This is done because stress can be faint in some areas while being quite clear in others. Physical, emotional, and mental symptoms of stress will be observed.

Physical Symptoms of Stress

Physical symptoms are the easiest to observe, especially from the outside. Common symptoms of stress include tenseness, panic attacks, tiredness, stiff neck, shoulder and backache, lack of or increased appetite, lightheadedness, rapid breathing, palpitations, high blood pressure, tingling in the arms and legs, insomnia, indigestion or upset stomach, sweating or sweaty palms, muscle tension, headaches, susceptibility to infection, rashes and dizziness.

Emotional Symptoms of Stress

Emotional symptoms are harder to spot as it is often internal, making it difficult to observe from the outside. Emotional symptoms include anxiety, despair, depression, frustration, irritability, moodiness, anger, crying, withdrawal, loss of interest, rapid mood swings, and loss of a sense of humor.

Mental Symptoms of Stress

Mental symptoms are the hardest to observe and are best done so by the person going through the stress themselves. Mental symptoms include impaired perception, reduced concentration, poor judgment, indecisiveness, reduced creativity, inaccuracy, and reduced motivation.

Other Behaviors Indicating Stress

There are some common and obvious signs that are directly connected to lifestyle choices and the workplace which suggest that an individual is stressed. However, it is best to consult a doctor because such behaviors can be caused by more than just stress.

The first and most important behavior to look out for is the use or abuse of stimulants. This applies to caffeine, nicotine, alcohol, or drugs as they are commonly used by those who are under constant pressure, because these substances provide the relief a stressed individual yearns for. An increase of use of this substance can be caused by stress and will only make things worse for the user in the long run. These substances will increase the production of adrenaline which, in turn, increases a person's stress response.

If a person is stressed, he or she will behave differently. The relationships between coworkers can be difficult and stress does not help in the interaction. Other good indicators of the presence of stress can be the reduction in quantity, quality, or promptness of work output. Other signs include poor timekeeping, working for long hours, an increase in accidents, dangerous behavior, and absence.

While levels of stress are objective, the response to stress is subjective. That means, everyone responds to stress differently. As demonstrated earlier, some people are happy (eustress) because a family member is getting married while some are unhappy because they have to attend the wedding and socialize with their relatives whom they are not so fond of. Therefore, there is a direct correlation between human perceptions. Two people can have the same event happening to them, but stress will fire up one person's productivity and confidence but will create anxiety and other counterproductive effects in another person. Here, if one knows how to use the power of perception, they can use stress to elevate their position and productivity.

Chapter 2: Power of Perception

Everyone involuntarily processes what they see, hear, and feel all the time, even if they have a great self-awareness. These stimulants influence how everyone makes decisions, sees themselves, as well as what they want to focus on. Every event happening in everyone's lives can be categorized into two major groups: positive, and negative events. What makes them positive and negative is the affected party's perception of those events and perception alone can change the outcome.

In the context of stress, suppose that two people working in the same company are told that there will be a downsize after the holiday. Of course, downsize alone is bad news for the employees and it is a difficult decision for the management to make. One person views the situation as a chance to roll up their sleeves and work harder for the company to make the best out of a tough situation. To prepare for this challenge, that person schedules their time for the job by choosing the right food to eat, exercising, and developing a plan, as well as reviewing their available options very carefully before coming up with the best course of action. Then, that person will follow through with their plans to find meaningful work, they will always be on a lookout for ways to grow positively for the future. That person understands that tough times will come by eventually, but they also know that small changes are sometimes needed to accommodate the bigger gains.

Another person, when faced with exactly the same situation, might have a different view. He or she may see the downsize as a path full of pessimism and hopelessness. Although they do not understand the situation fully, they made up their mind and just know that bad things will happen to them. As a result, they will become negative and their actions will be haphazard or even reckless because they no longer pay attention to details or do things that will affect their performance in the workplace. In shorter terms, they "stress" over the situation and they do not review their options and follow up with the correct course of action. They may forget to eat or take care of their health properly. All of this makes the stress even worse for them.

Which one is the best way to deal with a bad situation? Is it the first or the second person?

Human perception plays an important role in how we perceive the situation. This, in turn, also change the way people behave after the initial perception of the situation. While it is true that the problems will not just vanish into thin air just by thinking positively, it is also equally true that a person's behavior has an impact on their own wellness and the situation as a whole. Everyone should act and react in a way that, even if it does not make the situation better, at least prevents it from getting worse. The only way to make the situation worse is by stressing out, thinking and acting irrationally. Although not everyone can fully control the amount of adrenaline and cortisol they want in their body, they can control their own perception. It is a healthy practice to look for the good things in bad situations while keeping their views realistic. Doing so does not mean they are short-sighted, irresponsible, or unqualified to make major decisions in their lives. It is quite the opposite. History has demonstrated that, as long as the individual remains resilient, diligent, and persistent, good results will always follow even in the toughest of times.

It is worth keeping in mind that one should focus on or worry about the things they can control. Although one may not be in control of the entire company, at least they can secure their position in the company by striving to do their very best. How does one take control of their own perception and change it for the better?

Tips and Strategies

It is worth noting that taking control of the perception is no easy task. It will take patience, time, and a lot of practice. Everyone's perception is influenced by their past experience, and their brain evolves to process everything automatically. In any given situation, the brain will identify key triggers and perceive what is going on in a split second to prevent information overload. While it is a useful process, intended to limit the mental energy needed to navigate through daily life, it is not entirely accurate. Another thing to keep in mind is that, while these shortcuts are developed based on past experience, it does not mean that they are permanent. With enough effort, one can reprogram their mind to perceive things differently.

Define the Realm of Control

As mentioned earlier, one should first define their own border encasing what they can control. At the same time, they should know what is beyond their control. Everything should be very black and white, meaning that what is inside and outside the realm of control should be clear-cut. One might not be able to control their habit of eating anything with sugar in it, but they can control what to buy.

When facing a major challenge, it is best to identify what they can and cannot do. There will always be order in chaos. Sometimes, people shrink from a challenge simply because they do not know where to start. Rethink what the challenge can mean and find new opportunities. It might not be obvious at first, but a solution will present itself eventually.

Focus and Take Action

Once the uncontrollable are defined, ignore them. Put efforts and focus on what can be controlled. It is worth keeping in mind that good things are just as likely to happen as bad things. Instead of worrying about uncontrollable things, focus on increasing the odds of getting a favorable outcome by working on the things within the realm of control. Decide on what to do to increase the odds and then work on it, regardless of how bad the situation is, or what happened in the past. Now is the time to take control and act.

Let Ego Go

The best way to conduct a reality check is by determining exactly what is important and significant. It is best to prioritize things that are relevant to the situation at hand instead of the things that are beneficial to oneself. While it is tempting to be selfish and try to cash out before the situation gets any worse, one should actually turn back and face the challenge. Life is so much more than self-benefits. Do something that does not serve one's ego instead.

Reflect

Sometimes, in order to change one's perception, one needs to reflect on his or her own situation. Identify the problems they need to face, their fear, as well as the cause of their anxiety. Instead of seeing them as threats, view them as opportunities to learn and grow.

Most of the time, the brain is hard-wired into seeing the unknown as dangerous. This system can be traced back to ancient times when humanity lived amongst wild animals. Back then, mankind survived by avoiding what they didn't know.

Do Not Judge Immediately

To illustrate this, think of a time when something goes wrong. For example, think of a happy couple with four children. The husband is the one who provides for the family while the wife is the one who takes care of the young children at home. One day, the husband comes home to tell his wife that he just lost his job. The wife's first reaction would be to panic. After all, they have to feed four kids. How are they going to do that now? However, instead of panicking, the wife decides not to. She decides to panic a few days later if she must. She tells herself that she will only panic when the situation is bad. She opens herself to the possibility that nothing is bad unless she says so. Then, a few days later, the husband is offered a job that he likes even more that pays better and is closer to home.

Here, it is best to remember that the first reaction (that is, panic) is not the best course of action, even though it is instinctive. If it is unavoidable, try to panic a few days later. Panicking does not help the situation one bit. Imagine if the wife were to panic. What will happen? The entire family will be thrown into complete chaos. Relationships in the family will be damaged. Plus, with the damage left from the outcry, the husband might be less equipped to take on the new job. Even if he was not offered a new job a few days later, panicking still does not help the situation. It prevents everyone from thinking correctly and planning for the situation ahead. Therefore, the first thing to do is to remain calm. This is what many organizations or companies instruct their customers or employees to do. If inevitable, panic later. Remain calm, assess the situation, and try to resolve it.

Think Illogically

The human brain is programmed to assign meaning and value based on our own logic. That is why some people value one thing above others. For example, some people like animals because they are lovely, while others do not like them as much because of the mess they make. Both are right, and this highlights how differently everyone thinks. In order to change the way of thinking, one must think in a way that contradicts the established set of logic rooted in the mind.

This requires the conscious decision-making that feels illogical. That way, the logical flow in the mind is disrupted and begins to rewire. This, in turn, changes the established perception of the world.

A perfect example is Christopher Columbus. He thought

illogically by challenging the established logic that the world was flat. He was willing to think illogically and sailed off in search of the new world, even if it was believed that he would be met with certain doom if he were to sail to the edge of the world. As a result, he indeed found a new world and changed the perception of the world.

Look for Opportunity

When faced with a really bad situation, one should always look for an opportunity. If one were to focus on the situation, what would he find? Undoubtedly, he will find a lot of bad things and he will likely panic. Instead, ask what the opportunity is in a certain situation and how to make use of it for personal growth. By focusing on the opportunity instead of the situation at hand, a person could remain calm in the face of calamities which can result in opportunities. The answer or opportunity might not arrive right away, but it is always better than looking at the grim reality and become pessimistic.

Write it Down

Sometimes, the best way to think or experience something is to write it down. It is a good way to change one's perception. When faced with a challenging circumstance or condition without any solutions in sight, some have advised writing down the problem on a piece of paper or on any application in as much detail as possible. Place it on a flat surface in the middle of the room and look at the problem written down. Write down any solutions that come to mind until a preferable solution comes up. It does sound simple, but this practice offers a different view on the situation by taking it off the mind and putting it down on a piece of paper.

Be with People with Different Views

Since an individual's perceptions vary from person to person, the best way to change one's perception of the world is to be with those who perceive it differently. While one person may be impressed and overwhelmed by one thing, the next person might not share the former's enthusiasm. This does not mean that the way to change one's perception is by surrounding himself with those who belittle him.

When faced with a great adversary, an individual may be so stressed that he may overlook everything else. Having someone who has a different perspective can be useful as they can help the person to see the bigger picture by offering their own point of view.

Other Strategies and Tips

The most critical thing to remember about stress is that it influences thoughts, emotions, and behaviors. Therefore, managing stress is critical for a healthy life, both in the workplace and at home. While stress is largely uncontrollable, internal thoughts, emotions, and behavior follow a certain path that the person wants them to go. If the person views everything as a challenge, they will be more willing to face it in a healthy, positive, and constructive way. See it as a threat and the person will shrink away, avoiding and going off in a negative, destructive direction. It is entirely possible to modify one's perception of the world. The best example is eBay, where one man's junk can be another man's treasure.

Another thing worth pointing out is the fact that behaviors and thinking are correlated. For example, when a person needs to do a presentation in front of a large audience, he can think of the ways he could succeed by appearing confident. Just by thinking alone, when he actually does the presentation, his behavior will follow what he had thought in advance. If that person acts confident and knowledgeable while doing that presentation, his brain will think that he is actually in control and then he becomes less nervous. Since behaviors and thinking can be monitored and controlled, one can use either of the two to manage their own stress and pull through a difficult job successfully.

Chapter 3: Mindfulness

Mindfulness is a straightforward word that is so profound that everyone should know about it. It is an idea that the mind is fully aware of what is happening, such as the tasks at hand to the space in which the body moves through. Such an experience may seem trivial, except that the mind often wanders like a curious monkey. People's minds will inevitably wander, and they will lose touch with their body. Before they know it, they are engrossed in thoughts about things that just happened or worry about something they can't control about the future. All of those negative thoughts make people anxious.

To some people, the idea of mindfulness seems ludicrous. Some people believe that what gave them their edge was their unquenchable thirst for success, and that they know they can always do better. They are never satisfied with the status quo. Those that are always on the lookout for the immediate future without experiencing or appreciating what is happening now will soon find that, by the time they are at the end of the line – when there is only one thing ahead of them – they have nothing left to look back at. It is good that individuals have the drive to do their very best, to improve the world around them. However, they too should sometimes stop, look around them, and marvel at the things they have achieved while they still can. Those people hardly get any peace of mind when they ask themselves how or what could they have done better to achieve more. That question lingers in their mind all the time, and they can hardly find peace even when they sleep. Such a life is, while arguably productive, not a life worth living.

There is a good reason why greed and pride are two of the seven deadly sins. It is not a mystery that everyone always wants more, although they do not need more. Humans only need a few things. They need food, drink, shelter, safety, and a few other things necessary for survival. For a city life, people need a few more things, like electronic devices, electricity, clean running water, internet connection, etc. Everyone always wants one thing after another and is seldom satisfied with what they currently have.

In the modern, chaotic world, competition is always fierce. Those who strive to be at the top have to withstand a lot of pressure, which translates into stress. Some people love competition and they overwork themselves just because they want to be the best there ever was. However, life is so much more than chasing a higher position. What makes life meaningful is not the CEO title or that 10-story mansion. It is the fact that one can be happy and satisfied with what they currently have. Some people are so stressed about future work that they forget that they are currently having a lovely Christmas with their family. They forget to live in the present. This is where mindfulness comes in.

Mindfulness reduces stress and builds an inner strength so that people are more resilient against stress. Work-related stress and job burnout are some of the most common reasons why people have poor physical and mental health. Many workers subject themselves to the high expectations in the workplace, allowing stress, anxiety, depression, and exhaustion to manifest. Numerous studies have shown that there are benefits to mindfulness, such as increased job satisfaction, less stress, and anxiety. Mindfulness gives the ability to regulate thoughts, emotions, reactions, and feelings even in stressful conditions.

A Few Noteworthy Things about Mindfulness

Some people believe that mindfulness is an elimination of thought because bringing people to the present moment must mean eliminating thoughts of the future. That is not the case. Mindfulness is the awareness of all thoughts. This awareness emerges by paying attention to the present experience without judgment. According to the Cleveland Clinic, the average person has about 60,000 thoughts a day. That is a high number and it is impossible to stop thinking. In order to cultivate mindfulness in one's life, one needs to be aware of only a few of these thoughts without trying to stop thinking.

Practicing that alone qualifies as practicing mindfulness. It is the simplicity of being aware of one's own life as it unfolds, instead of worrying about what is about to come. Mindfulness requires constant practice if one seeks to reap benefits from it. Thankfully, mindfulness does not need a lengthy meditation practice or a yoga class.

Some people become intimidated because they think that mindfulness is something obscure or exotic. It is not. Everyone is actually very familiar with mindfulness because everyone practices it, in a way. It is not a special added thing that everyone does. Everyone is capable of being present in the moment. All they need to do is cultivate these innate qualities with simple practices.

Mindfulness is something so simple that anyone can do it. It cultivates human qualities that are universal and there is no need to change religion or lifestyle. It is that easy to learn. Mindfulness is also a practice that brings awareness and caring into everything people do, not to mention that it cuts needless stresses, even the little ones. What makes mindfulness practices a good idea to try out is the fact that there are benefits proven by numerous scientific studies that are positive for health, happiness, relationships, and work. Moreover, when people deal with the world's ever-increasing uncertainty and complexity, mindfulness can pave a way to an effective response to the problem.

Therefore, it is clear that everyone should operate under the mindful system. Not only is it productive in businesses or organization, but it is also good for individuals as well. So, how does one develop a mindful system?

Cultivating Mindfulness

There are ten easy things everyone can do in order to plant the seed of mindfulness and start living and achieving more.

Change the Phone's Background

An average person spends about 4 years staring at their

phone. Start by putting a "Breathe" on the background as a reminder. That way, the user is reminded to take a deep breath every time they look at their phone. While it may not seem much, taking a deep breath could alleviate some stress and allow the user to be present in the moment.

Set Reminder

Technology has caused humanity a considerable amount of stress in the workplace. Although it seems that technology has caused many distractions, it can be used in a productive way as well. It may seem counterintuitive because technology has made humans less mindful. However, by getting a bit creative, the power of technology can be harnessed to train the mind to be more mindful and aware. The best way to do it is similar to changing the phone's background. Try setting a gentle alarm or reminder to remind the mind to be present in the moment at least once every hour.

Change the Email Signature

Working with emails has become so boring that many people ignore most of the messages in it and change the part where it matters. The salutation and signature of emails have become almost meaningless. Although most of the email will be overlooked, try to use "With gratitude" as the email signature. It is true that the signature might be ignored, but it serves as a reminder as well.

Savor the Moment

One of the greatest tips to weight-loss is eating slowly. The same thing could be done here for a different purpose. Eating slowly is a perfect example of being grateful with what is already in one's possession. One could practice mindfulness by focusing on eating or drinking at least once a day. Instead of looking at the phone or TV, focus on the flavor of the food or drink. Savor every flavor. The same could be done when relaxing. Instead of zoning out and doing nothing, try to feel the moment when laying on the couch. During a vacation, take in the scenery and the fresh air instead of just taking photos and selfies.

Breathe

During moments when things seem out of control or moving too fast, take three deep breaths. In fact, the first thing everyone should do when they are emotional or losing control is take a few deep breaths. It allows them to calm the mind down and allow the emotion to blow over, therefore letting them make calm and collected decisions.

If possible, it is recommended to practice Diaphragmatic breathing. As the name suggests, it is a relaxation technique by breathing from the diaphragm rather than the chest. Basically, the stomach should rise up instead of the chest when practicing this technique.

It is a common practice for athletes to breathe from their mouth when they are running. Doing so forces them to breathe unconsciously from their stomach. Almost everyone is used to breathing from the chest. These breaths are often short and quick and only deliver a small amount of air to the lungs, resulting in gaining a minimal amount of oxygen to the bloodstream. Chest breathing often kicks in during hyperventilation or when the person feels out of breath because it helps to take in as much oxygen as possible very quickly. Public speakers are often told to breathe from their stomach because it helps them talk longer and maintain a smooth, deep voice. Everyone should have a habit of breathing from their stomach, since it also serves as a passive stress relief method. Stomach breathing uses the entire lung capacity, maximizing the oxygen intake at the cost of slower breathing. At the same time, carbon dioxide is also pushed out of the body at the fastest rate.

Diaphragmatic breathing is a good way to relax and reduce anxiety of various kinds. It is best to consult with a doctor before beginning this relaxation training exercise for those with medical conditions.

First, find a quiet and peaceful place with no distractions. Then, lie down on the floor or recline in a chair. If wearing tight clothing, loosen it and remove glasses or contacts. Put your hands in your lap or on the armrest. Then, put a hand on the upper chest and another on the stomach. Inhale slowly to draw in a deep breath. When inhaling, the stomach should rise up and the chest should not move. Hold the breath for a bit before exhaling while counting to three. The stomach should slowly fall back down. Then, continue this pattern for about 10 minutes.

Some people find it hard to maintain deep breaths for 10 minutes and their breaths often become shallow again. It is possible that the current practice is not a perfect moment for practicing diaphragmatic breathing. If that is the case, try taking a yoga class or sign up for a mindfulness meditation course. There are also voice recordings out there to help those who struggle with this relaxation technique. Their purpose is to help people fully relax and concentrate on the technique.

A good way to incorporate this breathing exercise into a daily routine is by setting up a reminder on your phone at a convenient time. The idea is to get into the habit of breathing from the diaphragm instead of the chest.

Appreciate

The best way to practice mindfulness is by focusing on being aware of the smaller, insignificant things in life that might otherwise be overlooked. While they may be unimportant, they do add colors to people's lives. This is a very effective practice that should be utilized by billionaires, monks, and stoics because it assists them to appreciate the beauty of life and helps reduce anxiety. By simply thinking about one thing that would be missed for not having it on a daily basis helps bring the mind to live in the present.

Another alternative to remaining in the moment that helps establish a bond with other people is by remembering that this time together could be the last one. It may seem a bit extreme or dark, but it is an effective way to encourage people to engage in meaningful conversation with each other. How much would that person be missed if they were to suddenly disappear one day? It is not implying that they will die one day, but the thought of not being able to talk to that person ever again after this makes people want to make their final moments together meaningful. This practice doubles as a helpful technique for those who have trouble sympathizing or socializing with other people.

Mindful Driving

Another thing that people tend to do mindlessly is hardly pay attention to their body when they are driving. Many people do not remember most of the details of their last drive. Such moments are perfect to practice mindfulness because a car serves as one filter from the noises of the outside world, not to mention that mindfulness allows the driver to focus on the road at all times – which is actually what they should be doing.

Next time, try to notice the steering wheel beneath your palm and feel the pressure under your foot as the car zips along the road. Use the lights as a reminder to remain in the present moment.

Mindfulness is a very simple and quick habit that many people can pick up. It is easy to personalize, and any techniques are effective as long as they help bring the mind into living in the present. It may seem strange at first because the mind is so used to worrying and calculating future outcomes that it forgets to be present in the moment. By sparing less than 10 minutes every day to practice mindfulness techniques for about 21 days, a habit will be formed.

Mindfulness alone is enough to reduce stress. As stated earlier, though, in order to change one's life, one must have a reason to do it. After all, while habits compel a person to continue doing something regularly, it is motivations that get them to take action. To many people, mindful practices for benefits of reducing stress alone is not enough to motivate them. In such cases, mindful practices could be linked to spirituality. It is merely a question of value for people when it comes to belief, but since spirituality is an important element in many people's lives, one could use it as a reason to start their mindful routines.

Chapter 4: Importance of Values

Values are, in a very broad scope, everything that individuals believe are important in some way to their lives. Their values determine their priorities and serve as a way to tell if their lives are headed the right way. Values can be said to be a ruler in people's lives because they help guide their behaviors, which ultimately determine their fate.

When people do things that are consistent with their values, such as obeying the traffic laws or following ethical conducts, they feel satisfied with what they do, even if they are not rewarded for their behavior. On the other hand, no matter how much they earn, they will feel guilty or dissatisfied when they have to do something that does not quite align with their values.

Types of Values

There are countless values, but they are categorized into four groups to help people identify their own values. Each group governs different aspects of people's lives.

Individual values reflect how people present themselves in life as well as their specific needs. It covers the principles people live by and what they consider to be of importance to their own interest. These values include humility, personal fulfillment, enthusiasm, etc.

Relationship values govern how people relate to each other, be they family, friends, colleagues, etc. Some people like to make friends with those who are honest, while others prefer those who are sensitive to their feelings. These values include caring, openness, etc.

Organizational values shine a light on how the organization in which people work shows up and operates in the world. It reflects the organizational value – what they prioritize the most. These values include productivity, teamwork, financial growth, etc.

Societal values reflect how people or organizations relate to society. These values govern how they interact with others in a society, and so these values include ecology, sustainability, future generations, etc.

Because values serve as a compass in people's lives, it is vital that everyone knows about their values. Defining values is more than just knowing them based on their own feelings. It takes conscious efforts.

Why Are They Important

Everyone has a different set of values that help guide them in their lives. They are important because they guide people's beliefs, attitudes, and behavior. People are not always aware of their own values. They help them make decisions that are right for them, such as taking a job offer.

To illustrate, those who seek stimulation in their lives seek exciting and new experiences wherever possible. They will go as far as taking risks for that bit of excitement. During a holiday, they will go skydiving. In a professional environment, they are willing to take risks. They take chances in their lives, not only because they are confident that they will win, but because they simply want the thrill of gambling.

On the other hand, people who give value to security and certainty look for comfort in their lives. They do not go out at night, and they look for stable employment. They make decisions only when they have as much information as possible. They can also oppose the changes in society in favor of a more predictable, stable one.

Here, it is easy to understand why the former group might have a hard time understanding the latter and vice versa. They cannot predict each other's choices, and it could lead to misunderstandings, distrust, and frustration.

It is worth noting that learning about each other's values can help bring people together. Because values govern people's behavior, understanding each other's values is needed for mutual understanding. One party's decision may seem right to them, but not to the other. With mutual understanding, they can bring everything to the table and able to reach a consensus. But what does value have to do with stress?

There are countless stress management techniques out there that require the change of behaviors, such as doing enough exercise, getting enough sleep, etc. However, so few of them address the benefits of self-disciplined articulation of a philosophical worldview and core values that help people withstand the devastations and tragedy in life.

Both Eastern and Western philosophies tradition recognize the value of self-reflection and self-awareness. Socrates once said, "Know thyself," and Confucius also urged individuals to reflect upon their values, how to implement them, life's missions, and how to attain them. According to Socrates and Confucius, management of complexity and stress rely heavily on self-awareness, ethical value system, and a capacity to act on core values in social relations.

Such wisdom does not really require validation from science, though psychology and neuroscience research has revealed how self-reflection manifests itself in a human's brain and behaviors. Neuroimaging research has shown that self-reflection stimulates the brain's anterior and posterior cingulate cortex that is linked to regions that regulate emotions and the decision-making process, proving that there is a direct connection.

In moments when one can lose their mind, stress can be managed or even prevented through self-disciplined contemplation of one's core value and goals. Religious people refer to such a practice as "Turning to God," while others say it is the turn toward their "best self". In any case, both groups work toward self-awareness diligently and maintaining a strong focus on goals and principles that are honorable and ethical even when they are stressed and facing uncertainties, risks, instability, and threats. When confronted with threats such as losing one's job or financial setback, people look to their true strengths and resources than losing their grip on reality. They accept the reality that they need help and seek it from their family and friends while maintaining an open mind about the next step, as well as developing a reasonable action plan to ensure that those who rely on them are well taken care of.

By attaining clarity of one's core values as well as a philosophical worldview can help individuals to develop resilience against chaotic, stressful situations. The use of contemplative self-reflection and the development of virtuous character traits help to remain steadfast against all odds. As a result, those people become leaders with more than enough capacity to do great things.

Developing an effective and sustainable technique to engage in philosophical self-reflection, includes regular journaling, reflecting on what is written regularly when convenient (especially when doing mundane tasks). Self-reflection helps to identify as well as reinforce self-chosen core principles, such as being humble, generous, gentle, and kind. Later down the road, they can draw upon their self-reflective stance when they are facing off against a crisis or stressful life event.

Everyone can reap benefits from such a discipline by practicing sustained self-reflection as a powerful tool to reduce stress. However, one needs to pause and reflect on their core values during stressful situations as a counter against stress. Before they can do that, they need to define their values first.

Defining Values

Similar to defining goals specifically to create a realistic goal, defining one's goals unveils what is truly important in one's life. Many people start by looking back at their lives to find out what made them feel happy and confident.

Identify the Happiest Time

Many people reflect upon their life, both professional and personal, to find a balance in their answers. They look for the time when they were at their happiest and examine that situation very closely. They find out what they were doing and whether they were with other people and who those people were, as well as other factors that contributed to their happiness.

By examining these elements, they are able to discover exactly what they did that led to their happiness and the actions that correspond to their core values. The company of other people shows whether there were people who witnessed those deeds, or whether those people benefitted from them or not. Finally, the other factors that contributed to their happiness are other variables that were also consistent with their values.

Identify the Proudest Time

The same as the previous step, people look back at their career and personal life. In this step, people try to find out the reason why they were proud, who they were with that shared their pride, as well as other factors that contribute to their pride.

The difference between pride and happiness is that happiness governs what people find pleasure in doing while pride is related to a purpose in life. Sometimes, these two overlap.

Determine the Top Values

While the previous steps ask "what?", this step asks "why?" Why is each experience important and memorable? It is recommended to find at least 10 values, and some of them may come hand-in-hand. Some people are proud of the success of their business because they were ambitious, adventurous, and enthusiastic. These three values often come together.

Finding these values helps individuals determine exactly why they favor one option over the other, which is very important in critical decision-making. By identifying the "why?", they understand that the favorable option might not be as logical as they originally thought. The more appealing option might not be the right one.

Prioritize Top Values

This is where many people have trouble because they have to look deep within themselves. At the same time, it is also the most important step because different options satisfy different values.

Start by writing down the top values without any order. Look at the first two values and contemplate if only one could be satisfied, which one it would be. To help answer this question, some people visualize a situation to reflect those values. For example, if they have to choose between stability and service, they imagine a situation in which they either have to sell their house and move to another country to find a better job or stay and keep the current job. Keep working through the list until the correct order of priority has been established.

Reaffirm Values

Finally, ask if the life and vision actually fit with the top-priority values. Here, people often ask themselves if these values make them feel good about themselves or if they are proud of their top three values. They also think about whether they are comfortable or even proud to tell others about the value that they respect and admire. Finally, they try to see if these values represent things that they would support, even if their choice is not a popular one.

That way, the sense of integrity and what is known are right, and the capacity to approach decisions with confidence and clarity is established when it is time to consider values in decision-making. Moreover, it reaffirms that the decision selected is best for happiness and satisfaction in the present moment and in the future. Making value-based choices is not always easy, but it can cut a lot of stress in the long run.

It is worth noting that identifying and understanding one's own value is not a walk in the park. Nonetheless, it is still an important journey that people need to embark upon. Consider it an equal to defining one's own life goal. Understanding one's own values is a self-discovery adventure. By becoming aware of these crucial factors, it could be used as a guide for making the best choice.

When faced with ethical dilemmas, in which all options go against some of a person's value, prioritizing personal values helps to make the best decision. The same could be said when one is faced with multiple options that are equally appealing to one's own value.

Chapter 5: Spirituality

Spirituality is almost as old as humanity itself. It is worth pointing out the difference between spirituality and religion because so many people use it interchangeably. Religion is the practices and beliefs passed down from generation to generation. Those practices are believed to be the communication between mortal men and supreme beings. On the other hand, spirituality is about the relationship between an individual and a spirit. Here, the spirit could be a supreme being or a representation of a human being's connection to a reality greater than themselves.

It is possible to be religious without being spiritual by simply following the practices and not believing in the supreme being. The opposite is also possible, by simply believing in a supreme being or a reality greater than their being, one can be religious without being spiritual.

Although it may seem irrelevant to stress reduction, spirituality has been a major part of people's lives. While some of the teachings are either unverified by science or outright lies, other lessons passed down are actually helpful. Plus, spirituality motivates and encourages people to lead a good life and generally be a good person. Here are some benefits people can take from strengthening their spirituality.

Better Decision-Making

Some spiritual practices are actually beneficial. People who adhere to a spiritual tradition may gain some health benefits because all traditions often pass down teachings about how to treat the body with kindness and avoid counterproductive behaviors. All traditions agree that lying, stealing, and killing is bad. Some even prohibit gambling or drinking alcohol, some of the worst things a person can do to themselves. Thanks to these tenets, people who practice a religion or faith tradition do not engage in unhealthy activities such as smoking or drinking. They are less likely to commit a crime or be involved in a violent activity. In fact, they are more willing to engage in preventative habits and are often eager to help other people who are struggling with problems like drug or alcohol abuse.

While faith seems vague sometimes because it asks people to believe in something that is hardly observable, it is undeniable that the tenets it has created serve as a valuable guideline for human behavior that remains relevant to this day.

Longevity

There are numerous scientific studies to discover the correlation between religious and spiritual practices and better health outcomes. An interesting study conducted by Giancarlo Lucchetti has shown that people with a strong spiritual life had roughly a 20% reduction in mortality. Such a reduction could be related to the fact that spiritual people consume a higher amount of fruits and vegetables as part of their self-care routine, not to mention that they are more likely to take medication regularly. While some researchers have disputed such findings, it is quite clear that there is a direct relation.

Here, it is worth mentioning that it is the healthy practices that extend spiritual people's longevity. However, they would not engage in such activities if they were not a part of the ancient holy teachings. This proves that spirituality can be a motivational factor for some people to start taking action to live a healthier life.

Forgiveness

Religion or spirituality also teaches people to learn to forgive. Buddha compared holding a grudge to holding a piece of burning charcoal. He who holds grudges intends to throw that charcoal at his target, but he cannot, and he ends up clinging onto it, waiting for the day to finally be able to throw it. However, the longer he holds onto it, the more he suffers. The only way to release himself from suffering is by letting go of grudges and forgive.

It is worth noting that bearing a grudge against someone is also a cause of stress, especially if that person is present in the workplace. By letting go, one is able to eliminate one of the greatest causes of stress.

Peace

Everyone spends so much time rushing from one job to another in a desperate attempt to get as many things done as possible. At the same time, they subject themselves to countless thoughts racing through their minds. Practicing spirituality allows them to find shelter from the chaos of the outside world. The time spent meditating, praying, or just appreciating what is around and within them in that moment is enough to create a buffer that allows them to truly appreciate what they have rather than trying to pursue what they want.

Giving Up Control

Sometimes, people try to seize control of everything, knowing fully well that they cannot. This causes a considerable amount of stress, not to mention that they are doing things they know to be futile. In such cases, it is best to believe in a supreme being and allow fate to run its course. There is a famous saying that one should take control of his own fate. While that is true, people should only focus on what they can control and leave the greater being to handle the rest, having faith that whatever comes next is justified and fair. Bad and good things can and will happen regardless of what people do. Some people do not understand that, and they often blame themselves for what they did not do. Spirituality can allow them to release the need for self-blame during bad times. It allows people to let go.

Finding the Lesson

Those who are spiritual have the added benefits of interpreting stressful situations as a challenge rather than an obstacle. In other cases, even when the situation is extremely difficult for them, they see it as a lesson from God. While their perspective does not really change the reality of the situation, they believe that they can overcome this challenge.

Resilience

Some people overcome some of the greatest traumas in life by finding comfort in spirituality or religion. It may seem strange, but it can be comforting to many people to know that there is a higher being looking after them and promising them a better day, especially during their darkest moments when they have no other people to turn to. With spiritual guidance, many people face their greatest challenges, bounce back from their countless failures, and carry on.

Being spiritual means so much more than just believing in a greater being. Having a strong spiritual outlook allows people to find meaning in life's complex, chaotic and difficult circumstances. Those people believe that life is so much more than just being rich and able to afford anything they want. They believe in being a good person and contributing to the community so that, when they leave one day, they know that they leave this world a better place than they found it.

By recognizing the interconnection of all life on Earth, one can numb the pain that comes with difficult and traumatic experiences. It is believed that if everyone can remind themselves compassionately during their darkest moment, when they really hit rock bottom, that their failure is normal and that they can always bounce back, then those dark moments become ones of togetherness and not isolation.

Many people tend to hide their painful experience simply because they believe that no one else would understand. They believe that, when they are truly troubled, they are all alone. This puts them in isolation which only makes matter worse. What they need to know is that everyone has been there at least once in their lives. That realization alone is enough to soften the blow.

It is clear that spirituality is very meaningful to the lives of many people. It makes life worth living. It makes life a lot more than a repetitive cycle of home-work until death. Spirituality allows people to discover what it means to actually live their life to the fullest and die knowing that they lived well and leave the world without regret.

So, how does one use spirituality to counter stress?

Spirituality and Stress Relief

As mentioned earlier, spirituality is not the only way to find God. Those who embark on a spiritual path will be able to find a community of supportive, like-minded people with whom they can grow with. There, they can find a great stress relief and meaning of life. Here are a few spiritual practices used to counter stress.

Praying

Praying gives the sense of connection with a supreme being, giving the prayer a sense of calm, safety, and a grounded feeling. These sensations serve as a buffer against stress. Praying gives similar benefits to meditation, such as lower blood pressure, strengthened immunity, emotional control, and much more. Praying does not need to be in a temple or church. It can be performed anywhere, as long as it brings inner peace and calmness.

Some people pray because they want to seek answers to their problem. It is likely that they seek answers from the deity that they worship. This practice gives the same result as writing a journal or talking to a colleague about one's own problem. Sometimes, the answer just appears when the mind is calm. Even if the answers do not make themselves known during prayer, those who pray always feel a deeper sense of trust. Praying gives them the confidence they need to handle obstacles in their way.

Gratitude

In spiritual practices, gratitude is often directed at the supreme being. Gratitude is linked with improved health and reduction of stress. Showing gratitude means not taking things one already has for granted, which leads them to take care of what they have better. Spiritual people often think about their health, which leads them to take care of it better. Some of them believe that their health is a gift from the deity they worship, and not taking care would mean insulting that deity, which is something they do not want to do.

Although belief plays an important role, and some people are not willing to believe as much as others, the benefits of being grateful is undeniable. An effective way to increase gratitude level is by keeping a gratitude journal. As the name suggests, everything a person should be grateful for, no matter how small, should be written down. Consult the journal when the dark times hit to give a sense of relief.

A gratitude journal is intended to remind people of what they already have. During dark times, many people often focus only on the bad things. Some are so obsessed with their misfortune that they slowly lose the good things that they have. Then, things spiral downward from there. The gratitude serves as a light of hope to those who use it. It tells them that not all hope is lost. It brings calm to them and makes them realize that, no matter how bad things can be, they can always cope.

Optimism

There is a saying that when God closes a door, He opens a window. Spiritual or religious people believe that God has something bigger planned for them, especially when they are going through a rough time. They remain optimistic during dire moments and they trust in the supreme being, their abilities to overcome hardships, and the belief that things will get better for them eventually.

Discovering Spirituality

It takes self-discovery to uncover spirituality. Just like defining one's values, it is recommended to take some time off and find a quiet place to start questioning one's own values and how they relate to spirituality. Think of which relationships are the most important, the top-values, the people that give a sense of belonging, what gives hope, joy, and what the best achievements are.

These answers help point to the most important people and experience in one's life, not to mention that people can search for their spirituality in their relationships and activities in their life. This, in turn, helps them define themselves and identify people that inspire their personal growth.

Cultivating Spirituality

Because spirituality involves getting in touch with the inner self, there are a few things to cultivate one's spirituality. The best way to start is by praying, meditating, and practicing mindfulness to help focus thoughts and give peace of mind.

It is a good idea to have a journal handy to write down feelings and record progress to give a sense of control over one's own life. Others seek out advisers or friends that can help them seek out what is important in their life because they may have insights that have yet to be discovered. Some people talk to those whose spiritual lives they admire to learn how they found their way to a fulfilling spiritual life.

Chapter 6: Meditation

Since ancient times, meditation had been used mainly for spiritual purposes. It had gone under the radar for a while until its reemergence in modern society as a means of maintaining stress and overall health. Although techniques vary, all try to get the practitioner to become aware of themselves and find peace, which has been the goal all along in ancient meditation techniques. The different techniques are there to accommodate unique tastes and preferences. The benefits of meditation are countless, and many companies have incorporated meditation sessions within working hours to help employees maintain an optimal level of stress for the highest level of productivity. Although there are countless techniques out there, all follow a certain pattern.

Benefits of Meditation

It is normal for people to view meditation as a fake practice, purely performed to capitalize on people's needs to relieve stress. One main argument is that there can't possibly be any good coming out of sitting still and breathing normally for 5 minutes. The doubts are justified, given how simple meditation seems. Because of the increasing trends in meditation, there have been numerous scientific studies conducted in order to unearth the benefits it brings.

One of the main benefits one could get from meditation is the reduction of stress. It is one of the quickest and most effective ways to minimize stress. In fact, a study was conducted from a sample of 3,500 adults, which proved that meditation does indeed reduce stress. But how does this work?

When under physical or mental stress, there is a higher level of cortisol and adrenaline in the body. Meditation serves as a way of keeping stress under control, mainly by telling the brain that it is no longer threatened and allowing the body to recover from the stress. With stress reduction comes the reduction in anxiety and associated disorders such as phobias, social anxiety, paranoid thoughts, OCD, as well as panic attacks.

Meditation is also used to increase self-awareness, which is vital if one seeks to change his perception of the world and address the root of their stress and behavior. People often go about their day facing the outside world while ignoring the world within. It is worth closing the outside world for a while and looking inside. Meditation goes beyond being aware of the fact that they exist, but also to help everyone contemplate their decisions and the lessons they have learned, amongst many other things.

Self-discovery is a product of meditation because it serves as a window for everyone to look inside themselves and discover their strengths and weaknesses and bring up ways to improve themselves. While it is arguable that one could do the same with a pencil and a notepad, meditation goes deeper into the mind and soul and people can discover a lot more about themselves.

Sometimes, the solution to their problems may be found during meditation. The solutions might even have been staring at them this whole time, but the clutter of the outside world prevented them from having a clear vision. Through meditation, one can remain calm and collected when they need to make decisions without having their emotions clouding their judgments.

Meditation Prerequisite

While one can meditate at their working desk from the outset, a proper preparation is necessary to get the most out of meditation.

Start by finding a good place to meditate. Any meditation veteran will say the exact same thing. A good place to meditate is where there is enough light, is open enough to allow air to come through, and enough space because meditation only really works when the practitioner feels the space around them is wide. Meditation in a cramped space will give off a suffocating sensation that hampers the meditation effects. Plus, meditation space should also be a place where the person can feel relaxed even before he closes his eyes. Decoration and color of the room help, but it is best to keep everything simplistic and clutter-free. Moreover, noise should be minimal to prevent distraction.

Depending on the meditation technique, a seat may be required. While there are standing and walking meditations, sitting meditation is the most practiced type of meditation and where everyone should start. Find a seat that allows for a body to rest comfortably on and relax without falling asleep. Self-awareness during meditation is crucial during the session. There are a few options when it comes to seats:

An ordinary chair is best for those who are new to meditation or those who have back problems. Since many meditation beginners often have problems keeping their back straight, the backrest of the chair is extremely useful as it helps take the focus off the back onto the entire body instead. Having back sores can ruin a meditation session very quickly since it may actually increase stress rather than reducing it. After becoming accustomed to meditation, using meditation is recommended.

A meditation cushion is commonly used by many people because it is the easiest to sit on in an upright position while letting the user remain alert. This also helps with posture as there is no backrest.

For those who are tall, have leg problems, or those who find meditation cushions and chairs to be uncomfortable, the next best alternative is a meditation bench. Just like the meditation cushion, it forces the user to keep the back straight, encouraging a healthy body posture. The only difference is the fact that the meditation bench absorbs more weight than the cushion, taking the pressure off the legs and allowing for a more comfortable and productive meditation.

The final tool needed is a timer. In a journey of self-discovery, it is very easy to lose track of time. Therefore, having a timer is handy and it is built into most phones. Set a gentle alarm as a reminder to stop meditation. It is not recommended to set a loud or disruptive tone for the alarm, as meditation should be a relaxing experience from start to finish.

How to Meditate

Since there are so many techniques, many beginners are often lost. They simply do not know what to do or where to even start, and the fact that some meditating instructions are vague at best only makes matter worse. Here are the patterns that most meditation practices share.

Sitting

The most crucial element of meditation is the practitioner's comfort. Therefore, the sitting posture hardly matters so long as it is comfortable.

Some techniques require the eyes to be open. Some people open their eyes during meditation to prevent them from feeling drowsy, which defeats the purpose of meditation. Some close their eyes so they can focus on themselves better. A good alternative is to keep the eyes slightly open and focus on a single spot.

Since most meditation postures help fix bad posture (curved back, slumped neck), the head should be held slightly upward and the back straight and erect. This opens up the body and helps relax. With the head held in that position, it also takes some pressure off. For the back, it is best to not lean against anything.

The same concept of what-feels-right in meditation also applies to the hands and legs. Place them in a comfortable position and stick to it. It might take some experimentation to find the best position, so switch it up a bit.

Getting into the Trance

Many beginners also have problems at this point, often caused by the lack of instructions. The most difficult thing here is how to control the attention, as most meditation techniques require the focus on only one thing. This is tricky because many people are so used to paying attention to many different things that the brain starts to seek out additional stimulants to fill the gap during meditation. Here, meditation challenges the practitioner to gather all focus and put it all in a single place (most commonly, breathing).

Start by getting comfortable. Find the meditation space, get the timer ready, and prepare the meditation equipment. It is also worth dimming the lights a bit to enhance focus.

Next, set the timer. Beginners should start small at 5 minutes and then go from there. Many people underestimate how difficult it can be to meditate for 5 minutes and go for as long as 30 minutes, only to fail in 3. Increase the length of the session only when needed.

Then, start the timer, close the eyes and the mouth. Take slow, deep breaths and focus on breathing. Again, focus on whichever aspect of breathing that works. Some focus on the sensation of the air entering the nose and filling the stomach as well as how it exits the body. Some focus on the sound. What is important is the pacing. Take only a few deep breaths to relax the body and then continue to breathe normally while maintaining focus. If it is hard to focus on breathing, there are alternatives to try out. Some people focus on a certain part of their body or place their attention on the light in the room.

While meditating, try to keep the mind empty. Do not think of anything. The attention and mind should be focused on breathing. Many beginners stumble here as they become distracted. If that happens, gently guide the focus back to the breaths. Do not become frustrated at the fact that the mind wanders. It's normal, especially for beginners. One trick is to count the breath when exhaling to help concentrate on the breathing.

At the end of the session as the alarm goes off, take a final deep breath, smile, and slowly open the eyes and allow the body to transit from inner-self exploration to the outside world again. Meditation is a process to develop positive thinking, so maintaining positivity even after meditation is just as important.

Additional Tips

Many have said that meditation is best done first thing in the morning and right before bed. That way, it is very easy not to forget to meditate on a daily basis and it helps to establish a habit of meditation. Just like a good exercising session needs a good warmup to prepare the body for intense physical actions, the mind needs a warmup at the start of the day as well. Meditation serves as that warmup or transition from a restful condition to a more active state. Again, a good exercising session also needs a good stretching to allow the muscles to relax. Meditation works the same way as well by serving as a transitional phase from an active state to a relaxed one. It is not advised to start off the day by abruptly launching from the bed into the chaos of the outside world full of stress, as the body will fail to catch on and become tired and unproductive. Likewise, it is best to end the day with a relaxing bedtime routine to allow the body to cool down after a long day of work. Otherwise, the brain and body will remain active and it can take longer to fall asleep.

During meditation, good and bad things will come to mind. Some techniques suggest brushing those thoughts aside to keep the mind clear. Some techniques suggest observing those thoughts from a third-person perspective. All techniques agree that those thoughts should be embraced in a kind, loving way and view them as they are.

Some people may become frustrated or even worried that they do not meditate properly when their mind wanders even for a few seconds. There is no way to meditate perfectly, and even the minds of meditation experts wander sometimes. The key is to guide the mind back and train it to focus on one single thing.

Meditation is more than just a form of relaxation. It is also a journey of self-discovery, which is also vital for the journey to change one's perception. It is important to remain aware of the thoughts during meditation since behaviors are influenced by them. Observe those thoughts in a friendly way and do not criticize too much. Because it is a journey of self-discovery, self-love and understanding are productive to the meditation process.

Meditation is a practice that yields great results for those who commit to it. Even the busiest person can spare 5 minutes to meditate. Just like the process of changing one's perception, meditation takes time before its benefits can be seen. Learn to develop a habit of meditation.

Common Mistakes during Meditation

Even though there are many ways to meditate, most meditation aspects can be personalized. Some people stick to the traditional practices and gain just as many benefits as those who spice up their sessions to make them more exciting. Though highly customizable, there are a few common mistakes people make when they meditate.

The first and most apparent problem has to do with the fact that they use too many props during their sessions. There are thousands of products out there that claim to increase the effectiveness of meditation or aid in the meditation. It is worth noting that these extra props are unnecessary, although a few of them actually help in the process. However, one should not have too many props because setting everything up can cause more stress. Meditation is all about inner peace, and external objects are optional. Keep the number of props to a minimum.

Along the topic of over-complication, meditation techniques should also be simplistic as well. There are literally hundreds of techniques out there, most of which have modern touches on traditional techniques. While science has contributed to these modern techniques, it is worth noting that they may lack the spiritual experience. Traditional meditation techniques have been developed and have thousands of years of experience in spiritual growth, which is important when one tries to change their perception of the world and address the root of their stress. Modern techniques are fun to try out and are recommended for beginners, but the traditional ones are recommended for the best effects.

Some people judge their experience. The goal of meditation is steady breathing and clear mind. It is meant to give the mind a break from the chaos of the outside world by creating a dome of silence, a sanctuary which the mind can retreat to in order to get that much-needed rest. At the same time, meditation is also a practice of patience and gratitude. It is important to keep the mind and heart at peace during meditation and many beginners stumble around this area. Many people tend to worry about whether they are doing it right, or that the meditation that they are practicing is the right one for them. Instead, stop worrying and focus on the stillness of emotions during meditation.

Guided Meditation

To those who are unsure of which meditation techniques to use or are just starting out, this technique is the best option. It takes inspiration from all other techniques throughout history and adds some modern touches to create a user-friendly technique. This technique is recommended for beginners because the traditional techniques require deep concentration and a lot of effort. In ancient times, that was not a problem because there were not a lot of things an ordinary person could worry about, not to mention that there were less distractions. Now, many people are not ready for that level of concentration because of the environment they grow up in. As such, guided meditation is created to help those people get into meditation. This type of meditation comes in the form of audio or even video, so a pair of headphones may be necessary as it helps isolate the noise as well as producing clear audio clues during meditation sessions. Guided meditation falls into four categories.

Traditional meditation provides the user with instructions throughout the process. Most of the time, no music will be included in the audio file and there is more silence than speech. The purpose of this meditation is to simply get the user to sit down and practice meditating.

Another form of guided meditation has come to be known as guided imagery meditation. This type of audio or video encourages the user to use their imaginative power to visualize objects, journey, or scenes that bring peace and joy to themselves. The goal here is to relax or heal the user.

Some guided meditations have music or natural sounds included in the audio intended to relax the entire body. Others have affirmations included in the audio in order to promote positive messages and thoughts.

Chapter 7: Quick Fix for Stress

Although mindful practices or meditation are some of the best ways to de-stress, there are other techniques that everyone can do in order to gather enough energy to push through the day. These take between 5 and 10 minutes.

Try to Engage in Physical Activities

Since stress is often caused by sitting and working in one place for hours at a time, try to get up and get the body moving. Engaging in physical activity is an effective form of stress relief. Some people might not even bother to do it, but according to the Mayo Clinic, physical exercise has direct stress-relieving benefits. Physical activities are considered to be a vital force in maintaining mental fitness. Think of physical activities as a way for the mind to switch from one task to another (as discussed earlier). Numerous stress-relieving benefits can be achieved just by getting the body to move and free the built-up tension in the body, mind, and soul. Do this regularly and the difference will be noticeable immediately. There is no need to go and lift a hundred pounds of weight in order to relieve stress. Just walking around for a bit is enough.

Physical exercise helps accelerate the production of the brain's endorphins, which makes the body feels good. Athletes describe this sensation as the equivalent to being high, which gives the sensation after physical exertion "runner's high". A rough game of football or tennis can easily trigger this feeling and reduce the amount of stress effectively. During intense games, one may feel excited instead of stressed. When jogging, the scenery and environment also keep the stress at bay.

When stress affects the body, the rest of the body is going to be affected as well. Therefore, it is safe to deduce that when the body feels good, the brain too must feel good based on the neural connection between them. Plus, scientific studies have confirmed that regular practice of aerobic exercise greatly decreases the overall amount of tension, improve sleep, and prevent mood swings. So, if possible, try to squeeze in some aerobic exercise.

Stretch

Even when the workplace does not have a yoga session or class, it is possible to create a yoga session right in the chair. Stretching sends a signal to the brain that triggers a relaxation response. A good way to alleviate neck tension and eye strain is by doing a neck roll.

Take a deep breath and bring the head to one side by laying it on the shoulder like a pillow and roll the chin to the chest while exhaling slowly, then move the head to the other side. Rinse and repeat to explore the tension in the neck. '

Walk

Consider this a continuation from the previous tip. Getting up and walking a small distance can help reduce stress as well. Sitting for long hours at work without getting up can cause a lot of stress, not to mention the tightening of muscles. Get up and walk away from the desk for about five minutes, allowing the eyes to rest, the muscles to stretch, and the mind to refresh before sticking the nose in the grindstone again.

If a lot of time is spent in the office, it is possible that the body may be confused about what time of day it really is, which leads to stress. Spending a little time in the sun helps reset the brain's internal clock and relieve stress.

Relax

Since many people spend most of the day staring at

papers, phone, and people, the eyes deserve a quick break. Turn away from the computer or other work and rub the palms together to warm them up before closing the eyes, and then place the warm palms over the eyes. Take slow, deep breaths for about 10 times and relax. Rinse and repeat as much as needed.

Alternatively, it is also viable to simply look away from the computer or smartphone screen. Prolonged exposure to the light coming from the screen can cause severe eye damage in the long run if one is not careful.

In extreme cases when things become overwhelming, it is best to simply shut the computer or put any task on hold for now.

Laugh

As the old saying goes, "Laughter is the best medicine," one can quickly unwind just by laughing or smiling. The stress will go away almost instantly. It is fun to laugh, and it is surprising that mere laughter can serve as protection from the damaging effects of stress. However, no matter how ridiculous it may sound, many people do not smile or even laugh often. It is even more difficult to laugh or smile during stressful situations. That is exactly why it is best to smile or laugh. Moreover, laughter gives a good boost to the immune system, making it more resilient, not to mention that it improves the mood and diminishes pain. The best thing about laughter (or smiling) is that it is free, and it takes less than 10 seconds before stress disappears.

A good, healthy laugh relieves physical and mental tension and stress very well, and it leaves the face muscle relaxed for up to about an hour. Moreover, just like physical exercise, the production of endorphin (the feel-good hormone) can be increased just by laughing, which eliminates stress and fuels the body.

Even when the laughter ends, the good mood remains. Laughing can help stop negative and distressing emotions. It is impossible to feel anxious, angry, or even sad when laughing. They do not mix.

The only problem with laughter is how to do it when stressed? Start by smiling, since it is the start of a laugher. When walking, look up and keep a beautiful smile instead of looking at the phone. Think of funny things such as comics on the Internet, and start enjoying it afterward. Try to hang out with people who are playful, energetic, fun, and humorous. Being with those people is also a sure-fire way to eliminate stress in seconds. However, if the workplace is very work-oriented and hostile, maybe it is time to find a new job.

Talk

Socializing with others also serves as a good way of reducing stress. That is why the talk at the water-cooler can be important to establish a good relationship with coworkers, as well as to relieve stress. While it may seem strange to share personal problems with other people at the coffee table, keep in mind that the benefits far outweigh the losses. It can be difficult to find the courage to talk about one's personal problem, but talking to a trusted friend helps in many ways.

Choose someone to be a consultant, such as close friends, loved ones, parents, or siblings. They may be able to suggest effective solutions. Even if they can't, just by talking about the problem takes it off the mind and reduces stress. Sharing a personal burden can help lighten the load and discussing it with a trusted friend can minimize the problem by giving it a voice that someone listens to. Most of the time, talking about it is more than enough to relieve stress. That is why most relationship advice points to one word: listen.

Voicing out the troubles aloud and explaining them to someone else helps identify the issue as well. Plus, doing so helps make the problem less scary and makes it a bit clearer of what needs to be dealt with. Keeping everything inside will only let problems build up and become even more confusing. Moreover, when dealing with things that cause stress, the problem is only seen from one viewpoint. Talk to someone outside the situation and they may provide another, which could potentially solve the problem altogether. Although stress is internal, keeping it inside and carrying it around in the head can cause physical tension, too.

Write it Down

Writing things down can be an effective way to get things off one's mind. Keep a journal about stressful experiences handy while going about to let the issues roaming inside the mind flow forth. Organizing thoughts in a diary or journal can greatly help facilitate problem-solving abilities and help eliminate negative thoughts and troubling situations that often cause stress. Plus, writing a stress diary helps you to remember what kind of situation is the most bothersome or irritating. Therefore, the stress diary also serves as a reference to help avoid future stressful situations. For example, if talking to colleagues or friends after class or work is stressful, write it down and try to find solutions for such situations. Moreover, writing a stress diary is an excellent alternative to telling other people about personal problems.

It is not really necessary to follow certain guideline when it comes to writing a stress diary. It does not have to be a detailed journal that contains a long story down to every single detail. Getting into the habit of jotting down troubling thoughts in a stress diary also includes writing things down on paper, laptop, or even typewriter. Moreover, having a stress diary is invaluable to those who do not feel comfortable sharing their personal problems with others when under stress, so they can talk about their problems when they feel like it. That way, the stress diary creates the opportunity to get solutions and advice from others and allow the problems to be solved properly. Noting stressful things down serves as a preventative measure and a stress-killing tool.

Music

Music can have a profound effect on the body and

emotions. Fast music can make the body feels more alert and concentrate better. Upbeat music allows for a more optimistic and positive outlook toward life. A slower tempo can quiet the mind and relax the muscles, soothing the mind and body and reducing stress. Music has such an impact because of the brainwaves that synchronize with the beats. When brainwaves are alternated, so are the rest of the bodily functions. Some of them are autonomic, such as breathing and heart rate. These functions are also influenced by music, with slower music inducing slower breathing and lower heart rate and vice versa. That is why people going for a jog or doing exercise often listen to upbeat or high tempo music.

Music is shown to have the capability of combating depression and anxiety as well. The uplifting sound of music, along with the messages conveyed in the lyrics, are routed into the mind to counter stress, resulting in higher creativity and optimism. Because of the numerous benefits of music, many hospitals use music therapists for pain management and other issues as well.

To combat stress, choose a tune that brings energy or any positive feeling. Listen to music while working. It is best to use music with a slow or moderate tempo because it is relaxing. Using fast and frenetic music could lead to increased stress by making the body hyperactive, resulting in rushed and hurried work. Some people, when stressed, are reluctant to listen to music, mainly because they feel like it is a waste of time and that they are not accomplishing anything by just listening to some songs. It just takes a small effort to start practicing this relaxation technique. A good way of incorporating music therapy into the daily routine is by putting together a custom playlist for certain activities.

Start by using music as an alarm in the morning. It should be a gentle tune but enough to wake a person up. It is not recommended that you use a favorite song, though. Some people report that they slowly hate their own favorite song when they use it to wake them up. Selecting the right music can help set the tone for the rest for the day. It is best to use classical or instrumental music, though some prefer upbeat music.

A common source of stress in the work day happens during the commute. A traffic jam or a bus arriving late is enough to stress a person out for the rest of the day. To alleviate this stress, use classical music or some favorite songs to make the experience a lot more enjoyable. That way, the mind and body are ready to take on the work waiting to be done after the commute.

When at work, put on some relaxing tunes to help the

mind relax and focused on the work. It might look strange to co-workers, but it is better than not getting the job done. It is best to use a pair of headphones to do it, though. It is considered impolite to blast music at full volume in the office or in public, as it can distract other people.

After work, it is recommended to eat at home to ensure healthy meals at less expense. Good nutrition is crucial to a healthy, stress-free lifestyle, after all. However, most people are too tired to cook when they finally get home. To encourage cooking at home, use smooth jazz or a similar genre of music so cooking seems like a fun activity instead of a chore. Plus, listening to smooth jazz sets the mood for a lovely dinner as well, making it something to look forward to after work.

Having a tidy living space helps cut down stress levels. Nothing is more stressful than coming back to a messy home. However, many people do not want to clean, especially after they come home from a busy day. Because they do not have the energy to tidy up their place, putting on some energetic music like hip-hop or pop can raise the energy level and make cleaning fun.

Finally, end the day with some relaxing music. Getting enough sleep is a sure-fire way to reduce stress the next day. It ensures that the body has enough energy to deal with tomorrow's stress, making it important for the proper functioning of the body and mind. However, because stress can negatively influence the quality of sleep, playing music while drifting off is a good way of counteracting the effects of stress.

Some music can also be used in conjunction with meditation because of its calming effects. Using gentle music with a familiar melody is effective but try to find music that brings a sense of calm, centeredness, and familiarity. Sometimes, it does not even have to be music. Some people find peace listening to the sound of a running river, wind chimes, rain, and more. Look around for what works best and use it with meditation.

To maximize the positive effects of listening to music, some people even sing along to the music. This works best for pop or upbeat music because it is a great release of tension and a great way to pass the time.

Pet an Animal

Some people are fortunate enough to have an animal companion in the workspace. It is not a secret that petting an animal reduces stress. Petting an animal increases the level of serotonin and dopamine, which are hormones that relax the body.

Numerous studies have shown that interactions with therapy animals may reduce stress. That is why emotional support animals exist. Petting an animal or playing with one leads to an increase in oxytocin (stress-reducing hormone) and also a decrease in the level of the stress hormone, cortisol.

When oxytocin rises and cortisol falls, the person feels more relaxed. This reduction in stress also has physical benefits. According to a study back in 2001, researchers found that patients with high blood pressure maintained a lower level of pressure during stressful situations when they had pets. There is also another study, which proved that those who own pets have a better chance of surviving at least a year longer following a heart attack, compared to those who don't.

Owning a dog, for example, can also inspire their owner to take them for walks. This form of exercise also helps to reduce stress in the long run because physical health is also related to stress. Those who do more than just walking with their dogs, playing fetch, for instance, also improves cardiovascular health.

Those who own cats or other pets can still benefit from

owning a pet because they make their owners feel less lonely. Because humans are social creatures, a common source of stress is loneliness. Animals provide their owners with companionship, which decreases loneliness and also encourages friendlier interactions with other people as well. Think of animals as a practice dummy for socialization. Everyone is comfortable talking to an animal, but significantly fewer people feel the same when they interact with their fellow humans.

As a part of mindful practices, animals help to keep the mind focused in the moment as well. When playing with pets, psychological health also improves by petting or touching the animals. Psychologists have found that physical touch decreases violence, strengthens the immune system, builds trusts, and reduces stress. Animals also have fun with their owners, making them laugh. According to the Mayo Clinic, laughter relieves the stress response and reduces tension as well.

Finally, animals increase their owner's self-esteem. A study conducted at Miami University and Saint Louis University found that those with pets have better self-esteem compared to those who don't own pets. This means that pet owners are less likely to be fearful and preoccupied, which means a lower stress level.

Play a Mind Game

Since human brains are wired to seek out negative events and memories, it can cause a lot of stress. This negativity bias makes the brain constantly replay the stressful events that happened a long time ago, making the current situation even worse. If that is the case, it is best to conduct a quick "brain dump" by eliminating these thoughts. There are many games out there, such as counting backward or reciting jokes. The best one is humming or even singing (quietly) a happy song.

Hug

A study has shown that only 5 minutes of hugging or 10 minutes of hand-holding is enough to lower heart rate and significantly reduce stress. Hugging is a great way to destress and it contributes to relaxation, trust, and compassion.

Scientists have found that hug therapy has comparable effects to some drugs, without the unwanted side-effects, of course. Even a meager touch or warmth can give a person enough strength to cope with emotional issues. Having a friend or a family member handy helps by giving each other a hug therapy.

Hug therapy is the use of hugs to provide emotional support or healing because it is shown that hugging is an effective way to treat stress, anxiety, loneliness, depression, and even some medical conditions. Because everyone is used to the warmth in the womb or being held as a baby, the need for that warmth by embracing remains even as adults. Because hugs are not given or received on a daily basis, hug therapy relieves stress by satisfying those needs. Here are some benefits of hug therapy.

According to research published in the Journal of Psychological Sciences regarding fear and self-esteem, touches or hugs have a powerful effect by reducing the fear of death. The research which was conducted by the VU University Amsterdam shows that hugging anything, even an inanimate item such as a teddy bear, can soothe a person.

According to Sander Koole, the lead researcher, everyone is aware that death will come around eventually. As the old saying goes: "It's not the destination. It's the journey," that makes humans strive to make their fleeting moments meaningful and memorable to them. However, those with low self-esteem problems often think that their life is meaningless. With such a mindset, hardly any aspect of their lives are positive, which is the main source of stress. They do not enjoy their work, and the things others find fun or exciting are not for them. To make matters worse, they might not be motivated enough to start mindful practices or meditation routine to find meaning in life again. Giving those people hugs can give their mind some peace by instilling some confidence and help them cope with the fear of mortality.

The need for touch and hugs becomes more and more important as people age. They do not get as much when they get older. Although people mature, and their minds become resilient, they slowly become more physically fragile which leads to the increased need for physical contacts. Because some people live alone, the loneliness that comes from aging has been shown to have powerful negative impacts on stress levels, which could lead to dangerous health problems. The sensation of closeness and warmth is associated with hugging, which decreases the sense of loneliness.

Researchers have found that oxytocin level is increased when hugging as well. Oxytocin is a hormone that promotes feelings such as contentment that could reduce anxiety and stress. When a woman is giving birth, this hormone is released to make her forget about the pain of delivery and allows her to show her child pure love. This hormone has the same influence on males as well by making them more sociable and affectionate. Oxytocin is linked to lower heart rate and blood pressure as well, making hugging also beneficial to the cardiovascular system at any age.

Hugging triggers the release of oxytocin, which calms the nervous system and boosts positive emotions. It lowers blood pressure, resulting in anxiety relief; it lowers cortisol to relieve insomnia as well as increasing the ability to socialize with others and gives a sense of belonging. Numerous studies have shown that a relationship tends to last longer for couples who hug regularly, compared to those who don't. Hug therapy should last longer than 20 seconds each time for it to have substantial benefits. Plus, another study conducted at the University of North Carolina shows that the heart is warmed when people hug.

The introduction of hug therapy in the earlier stages of life can have lasting effects. A study at Emory University shows a link between stress relief and warm touches. Babies that are hugged and loved when they were little are better equipped to deal with stressful situations when they are adults. The study confirmed the development of biological responses in the early stage of life.

Hug therapy helps regulate hormones in the body, including dopamine, serotonin, and oxytocin. When hormones are balanced, the immune system is also regulated, which leads to a healthy life. This balance helps the body to remain relaxed and more prepared to handle stressful situations.

Because hug therapy is so useful, it is recommended to introduce this into daily life simply by hugging when greeting a close friend or a family member. It is quick, easy to do, and has powerful stress-combating effects.

Acupressure

While acupuncture is a technique that requires the use of needles to pierce the skin, acupressure uses a gentler approach. Originating from an ancient Chinese healing method, acupressure works by applying pressure with fingers or hands on certain points of the body. It is believed that doing so can unblock the flow of Qi to release tension and restore inner harmony. The best thing about acupressure is that it is quick and does not require any additional equipment. This relaxation technique will bring instant relief if done correctly. Here are some easily accessible pressure points.

The PC-6 is a pressure point about the width of three fingers from the base of the palm. Put the palm facing up and measure. The point is at the middle of the wrist three fingers down from the base of the palm. Use the thumb to apply pressure until it starts to feel a bit uncomfortable. Do not apply so much pressure that it becomes painful. Keep the pressure on and gently knead in a tight circular motion for about 2 minutes one wrist at a time. The stress should go away. This pressure point also works to reduce nausea.

The HT-7 is the spot where the wrist forms a crease with the hand. Hold this point down with enough pressure for about 2 minutes. This pressure point helps to relieve tension.

The K-1 helps relieve insomnia, anxiety, and relaxes the body. When sitting down, cross one leg over the other and rest the foot on the knee. Put the thumb between the second and third toes and draw a straight line down until about 1/3 way down the foot. Apply pressure there and knead for 2 minutes. Do the same to the other foot.

Finally, the ears. Gently massage them with the thumb and forefinger. Because ears do not have exact pressure points, simply give them a relaxing massage. Pull down gently on the lobes and give the inner surface some attention. Do this for a few minutes.

Cry

Everyone has at least had a really good cry once in their lives, and it is often from sad situations such as a breakup, frustration at work, or something as little as a sad or happy ending in a movie. Among those reasons, most of them are caused by excessive stress. After crying, most people tend to feel a bit better about the situation. Therefore, crying can be said to be a good way to let go of stress. But how does it really work in a way that benefits the body and mind?

Crying cleanses the mind and body by helping the body get rid of chemicals that raise the cortisol level, which is the infamous hormone that makes people feel stressed. According to a study by Dr. William H. Frey II, who is a biochemist and director of the Psychiatry Research Laboratories at the St. Paul-Ramsey Medical Centre, found that crying releases toxic substances just like any other exocrine process, such as exhaling, sweating, and urinating. The chemicals present in emotional crying are protein prolactin, endorphin leucine-enkephalin, and adrenocorticotropic hormones that help reduce pain.

Plus, crying is also a good way to kill bacteria because tears contain lysozyme, which is present in human milk, saliva, and other bodily fluids that have the capability to kill up to 95% of all bacteria in under 10 minutes.

Tears also help clean up the vision by lubricating the eyeballs and eyelids, because when the eyes become dehydrated, vision tends to become blurry. Crying helps tears bathe the eyes, keeping them moist and washing away debris and dust. That is why when there is something in the eye, that eye becomes a bit watery.

Most importantly, crying helps to elevates one's mood and serves as the best antidepressant out there. According to a study from the University of South Florida in 2009, crying can elevate mood and sooth the body and mind better than any antidepressant, although a minority of people feel worse after crying, especially those who have anxiety or mood disorders. However, it is undeniable that crying provides a sense of relief even if the circumstance remains the same. Crying releases tension from the body and is infinitely better than punching a wall or keeping it all in, which could lead to health problems such as high blood pressure. If anything, crying is an effective and safe way to deal with stress by providing an emotional release of pent-up negative feelings, stresses, and frustrations, although it may leave puffy, red eyes and nose afterward.

Finally, crying improves communication, especially in a

relationship. Many people know that the true message in a communication is not in the words, but the actions. Sometimes, a problem cannot be solved just by dealing with it logically. Because humans are not robots, their emotions need to be put into the equation as well. There is simply no way to "talk" out of a problem. When a person bursts into tears, the flow of the conversation shifts toward the emotional aspects of the problem being discussed.

Lavender Scent

The scent is more than just a pleasant experience. Scents can help lift the mood and bring calm and energy. Using scents to improve health or mood is called aromatherapy, which is a form of complementary therapy. This therapy uses essential oils applied to the skin during massages or by inhaling through the nose. The scents from these oils, which are distilled from plants, stimulate the hypothalamus, which is responsible for the hormones in the body. Although different people have different preferences when it comes to scents, all of them have an influence on mood, metabolism, stress levels, and even libido.

Many scientific studies have shown that aromatherapy

can improve mood and lessen anxiety, especially lavender because it has natural soothing qualities that are believed to reduce cortisol levels, making it a handy tool to destress a bit during work. Therefore, try to introduce this scent to the workspace. If one is feeling tired and low in mood, use any citrus scent, like orange or grapefruit. Rosemary works too.

Breathing in any scent helps to take the mind off the frustration or the stress in the present moment. The mind wanders off from the current moment, which helps to destress. It is possible to incorporate these relaxing scents into the workplace through the use of essential oils, lotions, or scented sticks.

Chapter 8: More Ways to Reduce Stress

The above techniques deal with immediate stress relief techniques that take less than 10 minutes. However, if one is to truly have a stress-free life, they have to make some additional commitments. The tips below will require constant practice and a lot of preparation time. While doing them may seem stressful on their own, the benefits far outweigh the losses.

Time and Tasks Management

Nowadays, people lead busy work lives, and so even the most hard-working workers have to face deadlines that they might not be prepared for. This is quite normal considering that the workplace can be unpredictable at times. When this happens, things do not go so well and most often result in more stress than the worker is prepared to handle.

According to the Mayo Clinic, time management, when done thoughtfully and effectively, can reduce the amount of stress. Most people often commit a sin of time management by scheduling everything by giving it the same significance. When people do that, they tend to try to complete every single thing in the limited time frame without knowing that what they are doing is counterproductive and will cause them more stress and pressure. Proper time management is so important that some workplaces actually have to spell it out.

Plus, if there is a pile of work that needs to be done in a little time, it can be difficult to adjust the schedule. This is the time to be more realistic and think of what could be done and the importance of existing work. Doing so will allow for the organization of work based on its priority.

Since time is money, one should always try to be busy, especially when on a tight deadline. Therefore, distraction is a major issue when it comes to scheduling. To reduce or eliminate distraction, start by turning notifications off from social media sites. Disconnect and disable any Wi-Fi or Internet connection if the tasks at hand do not require going online. Keep track of distractions and get rid of them. Another thing worth considering is to eliminate distractive habits or minimize the amount of time spent on them if elimination is impossible.

One of the biggest mistakes that people make when trying to manage their time is scheduling every little thing and activity for their day. It is always a good idea to revise the schedule regularly, although accounting for every single minute is not a good idea. Meticulously planning every single thing is impossible. Doing so will be ineffective, and the irritation of planning, as well as the fact that things do not go according to plan, will cause more stress.

You should prioritize activities properly. Divide all tasks into four categories: urgent and important, urgent but not important, not urgent but important, not important and not urgent. Address the tasks in the first category first, and so on. Moreover, rank the tasks based on the deadline, difficulty, profit, etc. in each category.

When it comes to time management, self-discipline is the most important factor. Scheduling is easy. Most people fail when it is time to actually stick to it. Leaving existing duties neglected until the last minute will not only cause more stress but also affect the overall quality of the work.

Allocating Some Time for Breaks

Creating a schedule is good. Sticking to it is good. However, following the schedule blindly is not wise. A schedule should not be torture. It should have a healthy balance between productivity and relaxation. One should not become his own slave. There will come a time when exhaustion hits and that the planned tasks will go undone. Just like other machines, humans run on energy and overworking is never a good idea. Take Japan as an example, where an office worker could literally work himself to death. Do not be that person. Allow for some time to sit back, relax, unwind, and recover from all of that exhaustion, tension, and stress after a long day's work. Machines also have a work-rest cycle in order to maintain optimal performance. Humans are no different. Take a break once in a while to avoid being overloaded with stress. In order to maintain sanity and relieve the stress of their employees, some companies allow short breaks in the workplace. Try to make room for breaks.

Small breaks are enough to refresh and refuel the energy lost during working. They energize the mind and body. Sitting, typing, and staring at the computer screen for hours can take its toll on one's sanity by causing an insurmountable amount of stress. Some people, while understanding the importance of breaks, do not really know when to do so. The best sign to take a break is when the tasks cannot proceed because of stress and tension. When that happens, do small physical activities such as stretching, walking, or just standing up. Just 5 minutes of looking around and walking about can greatly relieve the mind and body. Taking a short break from study or work is different from goofing around. A break is meant to re-energize the body, mind, and soul.

Some forms of activity work better for some people. Therefore, try to keep track of what type of small breaks are effective in refueling the body. That way, it is easier to personalize the activities during the break to maximize the effectiveness of that 5-minute break. Sometimes, the deadline is so close that taking is break is impossible. In that case, consider switching focus on the on-going tasks by spicing it up. For example, instead of writing an essay, try to find needed data or pictures for the next presentation, or consult colleagues instead of working alone. Simply replacing one work with another serves as a break as well, because different tasks engage a different section of the brain. Switching to a different task allows a certain part of the brain to relax.

The main reason why vacations are so popular is the fact that it makes the vacation-goer feel like they are in heaven. Taking vacations is one of the best ways to unwind after a long period of stressful work or study. They have considerable benefits on physical and psychological health and wellbeing, which are directly linked to stress.

Relaxation Techniques

They are very effective in dealing with stress, but who wants to try any techniques when they are so stressed that they cannot even think properly? This is the reality and the reason why some don't even bother. Still, these techniques help in the long run, no matter how small or insignificant they seem.

Many people think that lying down on the couch watching TV with a bag of chips is a form of relaxation with psychological and physical benefits. This is not true, although it can be relaxing. However, it cannot trigger the relaxation response properly. Constant practice of relaxation techniques is needed to do that. The most famous relaxation technique is meditation, but if that is difficult or time simply does not allow it, it is also possible to practice a few aspects of meditation, such as deep breaths, closing the eyes, stretching, or stop thinking for a while.

Because there is no relaxation technique that suits everyone, try to find the one that works best for you. The only way to do that is by experimenting. If stress causes anger, irritation, or agitation, then a relaxation technique designed to calm people down is the best option. The most common technique is deep breaths to allow the time to think and for the emotions to die down. If depression is the product of stress, find stress activities that energize the nervous system such as power yoga, rhythmic exercise, or massage. If stress causes the body to shake or freeze, then running, jogging, or dancing are the best activities to perform.

In order to cope effectively with stress, it is necessary to create some time to practice a relaxation technique, no matter how long or short it may be. If possible, try to create a fixed time once or twice a day for relaxation activities. Since many relaxation techniques can be done anywhere and at any time, being busy is not a problem (or an excuse). Instead of the lazy relaxation techniques like sitting on the couch, watching TV and zoning out, try to pay attention to the sensations in every part of the body. This allows a different part of the brain to be stimulated because the focus shifts from work (which is outside the body) to the body instead in order to maximize the gained benefits.

Get Enough Sleep

One may feel unwell and distracted when stressed,

which can affect sleep. It can prevent a person from getting enough restful sleep, or even any sleep at all. Sleep and stress are correlated. Too much stress and sleep will be difficult. Enough sleep and stress will go away.

Stress is a common cause of insomnia because it makes it hard to fall asleep and remain deep asleep, therefore affecting the quality of sleep. Luckily, there are only a few things to do in order to get a good night's sleep.

Start by having a regular sleeping schedule. That means waking up and going to sleep at certain hours and sticking to it even if tomorrow is a weekend or a holiday. The worst thing to do to the mind and body is have an irregular sleeping pattern, which will not only irritate but also confuse and drain the mind and body of energy as well. Plus, try to get enough sleep. If the normal pattern is to go to sleep at 12 and wake up at 5, try to slowly increase the sleep duration by 15 minutes once every few nights.

Then, try to "cool down" before going to sleep. A person who has a difficult time sleeping needs a buffer zone, which is a period of time to allow the body to cool down and relax after a long day's work. That way, the sleep systems can kick in, making the body more prepared to relax and go to sleep. Try to start cooling down about 2 hours before bedtime. In that buffer zone, stop all work and end phone calls (even to family and friends) but allow for emergency calls. Watching TV is okay in the evening but try to stop looking at any screen about an hour before bed. Most screens produce blue lights, especially our TV and phone screens. The blue lights cause the brain to think that it is still daytime, and it tells the body to remain active, which defeats the entire purpose of cooling down. Many young people often make the mistake of staring at their phone for hours at a time into the night that when they want to go to sleep, they cannot. So, put all electronic devices away and immerse yourself in a warmer glow, such as orange light instead, which has the complete opposite on the mind and body. Reading or listening to music is a good way to unwind before bed.

Finally, make the bedroom look like a bedroom. It should be visually pleasing and comfortable. The bedroom should be the place for sleeping or changing clothes only. Keep all other clutter or as many electronic devices out of the room as possible. Other unpleasant and sleep-disruptive activities, such as working, talking on the phone, or watching TV should take place in another room. The bedroom is, as the name suggests, for sleep only.

Avoid Consuming Alcohol, Nicotine, and Caffeine

When stressed, people tend to consume alcohol, nicotine, and caffeine as a way to relieve them from the debilitating effects of stress. As depicted in movies and seen in reality, stressful individuals seek out stress relief by going to the pub and drown themselves in alcohol just to forget about their worries. They may think that doing so is a good way to cope with stress, mainly because they feel relieved immediately after consuming those substances. However, they actually have the opposite effects.

Caffeine and nicotine are stimulants. As far as stimulation goes, it only serves to increase stress instead of reducing it. Try to avoid or reduce the consumption of nicotine and drinks that contain alcohol and caffeine. Moreover, alcohol is a depressant when taken in a larger quantity, while it is a stimulant when taken in small quantity. Stress condition is determined by what is consumed.

The most widely used means of coping with stress is by consuming alcohol because it takes away one's stress for a while. Taking in a moderate amount of alcohol is fine.

However, people going through stressful situations often consume alcohol excessively. While a drunk often does not have a lot to worry about (because it is hard to even think in the first place), the hangover will cause more stress. In fact, those who consume excessive alcohol to avoid dealing with personal problems or coping with depression often say that they feel even worse after they wake up. Never consume alcohol to forget about problems. It does not wash problems away.

Caffeine is also a popular means of coping with stress, especially amongst young students and workers. Given the fact that caffeine is more accessible to everyone, regardless of their age, it can be found everywhere. Caffeine is found in tea, soft drinks, chocolate, and of course coffee. Caffeine is a substance that can cause many negative mental impacts if taken in high quantity, just like alcohol. Instead of drinking coffee or tea during stressful times, substitute them with herbal tea or green tea because they are full of antioxidants that are essential to dealing with stress. Plus, staying hydrated is a good way of reducing stress as well. Drinking water is fine, but for those who seek something with more flavor, fruit juice is a good option. However, if coffee is completely unavoidable (especially when that extra burst of energy is desperately needed), try not to drink it after 2 pm. Coffee has a half-life in the body for about 6 hours, so drinking coffee during dinner can really keep a person wide awake at night, ruining a quality sleep and the next day as well.

Movies often depict characters smoking when they are stressed. The same happens in real life, too. The damaging effects of smoking is not a mystery. Everyone knows that smoking is bad and is a reason for deaths by preventable diseases. Still, some people start smoking to reduce stress. The main reason is that smoking is tasty and addictive. Nicotine is found in cigarettes. It is a colorless, poisonous chemical used to kill insects and it can cause more stress, not to mention physical and mental injuries in extreme cases. Moreover, nicotine raises your blood pressure just like stress and it stimulates the production of stress hormone that results in more stress. The "relieving" effects smokers find in smoking comes from the addictive nature of the substance and it does not reduce stress. Think of cigarettes as a legal drug. It is a waste of money and should be avoided at all costs.

Therefore, these three substances are dangerous to consume. Alcohol and caffeine *may* be consumed if unavoidable, and should that happen, try to keep the amount to a minimum. Avoid nicotine by stopping smoking. Even consuming each of them once in a while is still harmful, especially when they are consumed to reduce stress.

Maintain a Healthy Diet

On the topic of drinks, food should also be addressed. When people are busy and stressed, they do not want to spend too much time making decisions, especially when a deadline approaches. This leads to poor nutritional choices that have an impact on stress levels, not to mention causing other problems. Stressed individuals tend to go for pre-packaged food because it is simpler, although it is not as healthy. Other people simply prefer the taste of less healthy food when they are stressed. Worse still, some skip a meal altogether and fill it with unhealthy snacks.

Whatever the case may be, having an unhealthy diet has both short- and long-term consequences. Those who eat unhealthy foods report having less energy, which affects their productivity and increases stress. The lack of energy also weakens the immune system, making them more susceptible to diseases, and it could lead to a lower quality of life. This leads to short-temper and mood swings that could negatively impact relationships with other people. Therefore, it is crucial to maintain a healthy diet. Here are some ways to do so.

At the start of the day, it is recommended that you do not skip breakfast. There are many reasons why people skip breakfast. Perhaps they do not feel hungry. Perhaps lunch will come around soon anyway. Maybe they are on a diet. Maybe that milk in the latte is all the nutrition a person needs to start the day. Whatever the reason may be, skipping breakfast makes it harder to maintain a stable blood sugar level, which affects how the body functions in a busy morning. It is not hard to grab a quick, healthy meal before heading out. If preparing breakfast in the morning is hard, try to do it at night. The same could be said for lunches. So many people opt for less healthy options simply because it is cheaper and faster. Preparing food from home is a lot healthier and cheaper as well, even if this is done only a few days a week. It is a great improvement over eating every lunch out.

For those who love coffee, it is time to drink something healthier. While the effects of coffee are discussed, an alternative has not been discussed yet. It is best to reduce the stress levels and improve mental health throughout the day by weaning off of a large amount of caffeine gradually and replacing it with decaffeinated green tea. Green tea has a soothing taste, not to mention loads of antioxidants.

The same applies to those who love cola, who have most likely experienced the same health consequences from caffeine. The best alternative is to try drinking sparkling fruit juice or sparkling water. That way, the refreshing treat is still there, and enough water will make it into the system nonetheless.

When it comes down to snacks, having some that are rich in protein in the car, office, or purse can help regulate the blood sugar level and prevent mood swings and fatigue. Try to eat trail mix, granola bars, or energy bars that have good nutrition. Also, have some water handy when snacking. To those who often snack at a certain time of the day or when they are stressed, consider replacing chips, cheese puffs, or other unhealthy munchies with carrot sticks, celery sticks, sunflower seeds, edamame, or other healthier choices. Popcorn works as well, as long as there is no butter and salt.

Some people struggle to stop themselves from eating unhealthy food simply because of how great it tastes. Perhaps the problem lies in the fact that they are available in their home. Get rid of most, if not all, the unhealthy food to allow the body a chance to snack on healthy snacks instead. On that topic, try to get as much healthy food in as possible. Plan a menu of healthy meals and snacks at the beginning of each week and list down the ingredients needed. Shop for them once a week. Some people are tempted to buy unhealthy snacks while they are out shopping. A good way to combat this temptation is by having a friend along to remind them not to buy unhealthy food. By planning meals out in advance, the stress of what to eat each night is also eliminated.

If All Else Fails, Seek a Specialist

If stress is so high that leading a happy and rewarding life is beyond control, and the situation does not get better even after all of the above has been tried, then perhaps it is time to consult a licensed professional. Trained counselors and health professionals, though individuals or group consultations, can strengthen people's management skills. For those who are abusing drugs or alcohol to counter stress, it is best if they stop doing so and seek help from a specialist for better solutions. There are many cases of stress when the only solution available is to visit a professional.

When stress is left untreated for too long, it will develop into chronic stress in extreme cases. Chronic stress is considered to be one of the most harmful mental issues. In such cases, it is time to have a specialist check for mental illness. A trained professional is able to provide effective measures for chronic stress, such as talking treatments, medication, complementary, and alternative therapies. For example, a stress specialist usually conducts a careful interview during which the professional carefully inquires what the root cause of the patient's stress is and what is making it worse. The sooner the treatment is addressed with a licensed professional, the better.

Chapter 9: Progressive Muscle Relaxation

Progressive muscle relaxation is a deep meditation that operates under the assumption that the muscles tense up in response to stressful thoughts. By relaxing the muscles, it is possible to release the built-up stress inside as well. It is also an effective way to relieve insomnia and reduce symptoms of certain types of chronic pain.

This relaxation technique works to counter the infamous fight-or-flight reaction that causes a lot of stress. This response is a common reaction to fear or danger, which is hardly the case in reality. Nowadays, harmless situations can trigger this response and it triggers physical symptoms such as accelerated heart rate, sweating, shaking, and shortness of breath thanks to the stress hormones. Since muscle pain, stiffness, and tension are common symptoms of stress and anxiety, this relaxation relieves stress by addressing those symptoms. It forces a relaxation response, calming the mind and lowering the heart rate by practicing slow, deep breathing and muscle relaxation routines.

This technique was described by Edmund Jacobson in about 1930. It is based upon his premise that mental calmness is a natural result of physical relaxation. Progressive muscle relaxation is very easy to learn and only requires 10 to 20 minutes a day to practice. While these techniques are effective against a wide number of conditions, some of which cannot be treated by medicine, it is worth noting that it can take a lot of therapy sessions to complete.

Progressive muscle relaxation is useful for treating conditions that medicine fails to cure, such as dementia. Even if the condition can be treated, some people prefer practicing these techniques rather than taking medicine, because there is little or no risk associated with them. These techniques serve as a useful supplementary treatment for some psychological conditions as well. It is shown to be effective against withdrawal symptoms such as craving.

PMR: Step by Step

Start by finding a quiet place free from distractions. Lie down on the floor or recline in a chair. Loosen any tight clothing and remove glasses or contacts. Put your hands in your lap or on the armrest. Then, take in a few deep breaths slowly. It is recommended to do a diaphragmatic breathing exercise throughout the entire exercise by synchronizing the breaths with the tension and the relaxation of the muscle in each area, but do not hold the breath. Some people find it more comfortable to work from the top of their head down to their toes. Others prefer doing it in the opposite direction. While this guide follows the former direction, it is still applicable to the latter method. Just like meditation, it is important to focus on each area of the muscle as it tightens and relaxes. It is okay if the mind wanders. Just guide it back to the muscle and proceed normally. Another thing worth noting is that one should not tighten the muscles.

Starting with the forehead muscle by raising the brows as high as possible, hold for about 5 seconds and then quickly release that tension. Give it a 5 to 10 second break and then move on to the cheek muscle. Smile as widely as possible. The mouth and cheeks should feel tense. Hold for 5 seconds and release quickly again. Do the same with the head by gently pulling it back to look at the ceiling, hold, release, and pause.

Moving down to the hand, clench the right fist, hold, release, and pause. Do the same to the right forearm, the upper arm, and then the entire arm. Make sure that the muscle in each area is tightened and feel the tension and relaxation. Do the same for the shoulders by lifting them as high as possible. Repeat the process for the left hand, and then do the shoulders again.

Then, tense the upper back by pulling the shoulders back, hold, release, and pause. Work on the lower back by arching it. Then, do the same for the buttocks. After that, work on the legs by first tensing the entire right leg and thigh. Pull the toes inside and feel the tension in the calves. Repeat for the left leg.

Finally, bring the entire relaxation session to a close by feeling a wave of relaxation going from the head to toe. Relax and breathe slow and deep breaths for a few minutes.

Chapter 10: Social Support

Because loneliness is associated with a large number of health problems, such as weakened immune systems, cognitive decline, cardiovascular disease, and high blood pressure, having a strong social support is needed in a healthy life. Thankfully, there are many ways to seek out such support and nurture supportive relationships.

Benefits of Social Support

Having strong social support is important, although many people do not feel that they have access to such a valuable resource. When they are asked if they have someone to turn to for emotional support, such as talking about their personal problems or helping them make difficult decisions, most of them said yes. However, almost half of them said they could benefit from having a bit more emotional support.

According to experts, almost everyone benefits from social and emotional support. While it may seem counterintuitive at first, having a strong social support helps a person cope with problems on their own by improving their self-esteem and sense of autonomy.

Thankfully, there is no need for a large network of friends and family in order to benefit from social support. A bunch of people is enough so long as there is enough emotional and social support from them. However, it takes social skills in order to form a social support, and they do not always come naturally. Some have problems making social connections while others lose established connections because of life changes, such as moving away, retirement, relocation, or the death of a loved one. Still, it is possible to create new connections and reap the benefits of a healthy support network.

Types of Social Support

There are different types of social support for different situations. Of course, they have unique benefits, and it is recommended to have all four types of social support.

Emotional Social Support

This type includes affirmations of one's worth, sharing of positive regards, and a concern about one's feelings.

People in this network should be able to listen to the troubled one and validate their feelings, letting them know that they are valued as well as offering a shoulder to cry on.

Informational Social Support

This network involves the sharing of information or advice to help the troubled one to overcome a challenge or to help them make a decision. The people in this network should be able to offer useful advice or point to experts that can offer advice as well as share their personal experience relating to the problem.

Tangible Social Support

This network includes sharing resources such as money. Of course, this can also mean providing loans or monetary gifts. Offering to share childcare duties, helping a friend move, or even bringing a casserole to a grieving family also counts as tangible social support.

Belonging Social Support

This network involves providing social leisure and

belonging, such as being friends in the group and spending time with friends who need support.

Nurturing the Social Network

Start by casting a wide net because not everyone is capable of providing emotional and social support in all circumstances. A colleague might listen to work problems, but only the neighbors can listen to difficulties with the kids. Find different relationships for different kinds of support, but make sure that people are trustworthy to avoid disappointment or negative interactions that could lead to more stress.

Most of the time, people expect others to reach out to them, only to feel rejected when people do not go out of their way to do so. In order to get the most out of any social relationships, one has to make an effort. When writing a schedule, leave some room to interact with friends and family. Reach out to them to lend a hand or simply saying hello is good enough sometimes. People in the social support network will be more likely to lend support when they feel the connection. In fact, research suggests that providing social support to friends and family is more important than receiving it.

Although face-to-face conversation is good, not many people have the time for that. Thanks to the advancement of technology, it is now a lot easier to reach out to other people, especially when they are far away. Send a text message asking how they are doing, write an email, or arrange a date for a video chat to stay connected. Because of its simplicity and convenience, some people tend to rely too much on technology. Therefore, try not to overuse it.

Another way to expand the social support network is by connecting with people who have similar interests. Join a club, volunteer, sign up for a class, or attend any events where likeminded individuals meet. Do not be discouraged if things are off to a slow start. Instead, try to enjoy the experience. In some cases, the support needed might not be in the current, established network. Then, consider joining a support group to meet others that share similar challenges.

Sometimes, improving social skills is all that is needed to expand the network. Some people find it hard to socialize with others and do not know what to say, making the interaction seem awkward. A good trick shy people employ is by getting to know others through shared interests such as knitting class, yoga, etc. This works because everyone is in a comfortable environment, even for introverts, and it is easier to get to know one another than just hanging out and talking.

Chapter 11: Common Mistakes During Stress

Mistakes happen when people become frustrated. It is normal because people tend to lose control of what they are doing when under pressure. If they are in control of themselves, then there is no such thing as being stressed out by the demands from their surroundings. Those mistakes impact their lives by making them a lot more difficult and complicated than they should be, even when stress is gone. Such mistakes usually have after-stress effects that worsen the situation during stressful situations.

Some mistakes are more common for a majority of people than others. While they seem insignificant, they have a devastating effect on people's lives. Here are some of the most common mistakes made during stress and how to avoid them.

Making Hasty Decision

There is a saying that one should not make a decision when one is angry. This is the most common mistakes that people make. When under pressure, people always make instantaneous decisions based on their feelings without thinking twice about it. Most of the time, they will make a wrong decision. But what is the relationship between stress and anger? Sometimes, people are so stressed that even the smallest problem can make them frustrated.

Every now and then, people make hasty decisions when they are under pressure. Those decisions are not always perfect, and most of the time they are wrong decisions that contribute to negative effects on their lives after that. When people are anxious, their critical thinking starts to plummet. Their chances of making the right decision and thinking carefully are very low.

The human brain cannot function properly because there are many things happening in it at the same time. People's rash decisions may result in many other negative effects in the aftermath of the stressful situations. Therefore, consider thinking thoroughly before acting. It will help in making the best option that can, in turn, be the right choice.

Procrastinate

It is obvious that many people sometimes (or most of the

time) are not in the mood to do anything when they are stressed out. At the same time, it is also known that procrastination can happen to everyone, even though they are not under pressure. However, according to numerous studies and statistics, people who are under a lot of pressure tend to have a higher chance of putting off work compared to those who are not stressed. Stress disturbs people's ability to think. When their brain and thinking ability are disturbed, they tend to procrastinate and become lazy because they are led to believe that now is not the right time to complete the task yet, simply because they don't feel like it.

Procrastination affects everyone who is under stress. People who procrastinate are more stressed than those who are committed to working under pressure. These two are very different things. Procrastinators delay doing the tasks until the very last moment in which they have to rush everything. Thus, it puts them in a more stressful situation than before because the deadline draws near. On the other hand, people who are still committed to work under pressure can manage their tasks properly and have more time to manage everything. Working under pressures here does not mean that they work nonstop. They still have time for themselves to relax after a long working hour.

Isolation

When under stress, people tend to occupy themselves with anti-social behavior. This restricts them from doing any fun activities that are actually helpful in reducing stress. They think that involving themselves with group activities will cause them more stress. However, cutting themselves out of any fun activities like this is a bad way to handle stress. Isolation does not help to reduce stress. Instead, it will build up and explode when the limit is reached. The worst thing people can do to themselves is put themselves in an isolated position. Doing so will allow depression and suicidal thoughts to appear, which is very dangerous. Isolation is the biggest mistake that many people make when they are stressed.

Taking No Break

As discussed earlier, the body needs to have a break, especially after a long day of work. Many people underestimate the importance of allowing their body to rest. They neglect sleeping or taking breaks, and such behavior can cause major damage to physical and mental health by putting the body under more stress than it can handle. The body needs time to relax and recharge after having been hard at work throughout the day. Overexertion forces the body to take the extra energy from another part of the body and deteriorates health, making the body more susceptible to illness.

Not Accepting Reality

Though ludicrous, some people actually commit this mistake that worsens their stress. They do not accept the reality that they are not stressed. They believe that pressure does not exist. They think that the stressful situations they are going through now are normal and are a fact of life. Now acknowledging the fact that one is under stress does not help increase productivity. There is no way to fool one's own body. It knows what it is going through, and it is going to respond accordingly. What is an illusion is the thought that, by not thinking that they are under stress, it will go away. This is wrong on so many levels. Some people with this belief will work without breaks and cause their body to reach a complete shutdown state.

Conclusion

To conclude, stress is a normal part of life. However, the fact that it impedes performance in the workplace and influences people's lives negatively brings about the need to get it under control. Fortunately, there are traditional and modern techniques to combat stress, and some of them are quick and easy to do whereas others are formed by constant practice that yield lasting results.

Although stress seems bad, maintaining an optimal level is recommended for maximum productivity and creativity. Incorporating relaxation techniques into the daily routine is the best way to enhance one's overall quality of life. However, some people may find it hard to remain motivated to keep up with all the necessary exercises.

It is true that the countless techniques discussed in this book are only effective when people actually put them to practice. A good motivator, of course, comes from within. By changing one's perception of everyday situations, practicing mindfulness techniques, as well as finding one's values, it is possible to finally become motivated to start living a healthy life.

www.ingramcontent.com/pod-product-compliance
Lightning Source LLC
Chambersburg PA
CBHW070109080526
44586CB00013B/1240